17th Industrial Conference on Advances in Data Mining (ICDM 2017)

Poster Proceedings

New York, New York, USA
12-13 July 2017

Editors:

Petra Perner

ISBN: 978-1-5108-9514-0

Printed from e-media with permission by:

Curran Associates, Inc.
57 Morehouse Lane
Red Hook, NY 12571

CURRAN ASSOCIATES INC. proceedings.com

Some format issues inherent in the e-media version may also appear in this print version.

ibai-publishing
Arno-Nitzsche-Str. 45
04277 Leipzig, Germany

info@ibai-publishing.org

Additional copies of this publication are available from:

Curran Associates, Inc.
57 Morehouse Lane
Red Hook, NY 12571 USA
Phone: 845-758-0400
Fax: 845-758-2633
Email: curran@proceedings.com
Web: www.proceedings.com

Table of Content

Petra Perner (Ed.)

Advances in Data Mining

17th Industrial Conference, ICDM 2017
New York, USA, July 2017

Poster Proceedings

ibai Publishing
www.ibai-publishing.org

Petra Perner (Ed.)

Advances in Data Mining

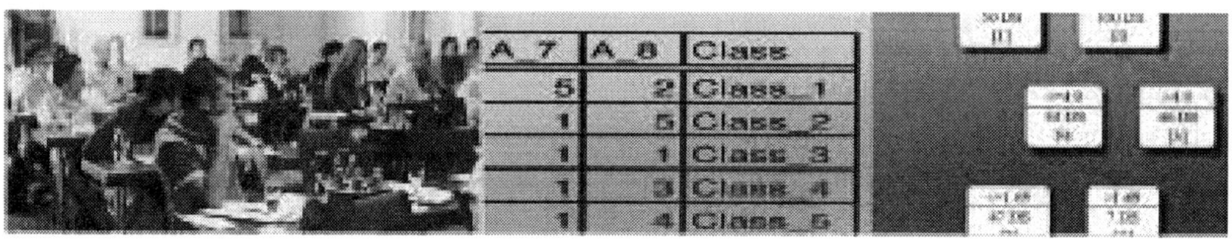

17th Industrial Conference, ICDM 2017
New York, July 2017

Workshop Proceedings

ibai - publishing

The German National Library listed this publication in the German National Bibliography.
Detailed bibliographical data can be downloaded from http://dnb.ddb.de.

Creating Patent Maps with Self-Organizing Maps for Corporate Decision Making on R&D of New Products

Kazuhiro Kohara and Tomonori Ito

Chiba Institute of Technology
2-17-1 Tsudanuma, Narashino, Chiba 275-0016, Japan
kohara.kazuhiro@it-chiba.ac.jp

Abstract. Previously, we proposed an approach for corporate decision making with self-organizing patent maps labeled by technical terms and AHP. First, we extracted keywords by text mining to transform patent documents into feature vectors of the companies. Second, we inputted the feature matrix of technical terms and company names into self-organizing maps to create patent maps labeled by the technical terms. Then, we considered several corporate strategies utilizing the patent maps and made a decision with AHP. In previous papers, we used all documents applied for a patent in Japan and self-organizing patent maps labelled by technical terms. In this paper, we consider several corporate strategies on R&D of new products using two types of patent maps labeled by technical terms and company names. We applied our approach to patent area of information home appliance and home network. We used only registered patents to show examples of considering corporate strategies and decision making with AHP.

Keywords: business intelligence, technology marketing, decision making, corporate strategy, new products, patent maps, self-organizing maps, text mining, AHP

1 Introduction

When a company starts research and development or licensing for entering into a new business in a certain technology field, the company needs to recognize the overall scope of that and other related technology fields, including pertinent patents. A patent map is the visualized expression of total patent analysis results for understanding complex patent information easily and effectively. The patent map is produced by gathering, processing, and analyzing pertinent patent information of the targeted technology field. Creating and updating such a map requires substantial human effort. Because automatic tools for assisting patent analysis are in demand, patent documents are typically analyzed by text mining, which is a technique for finding hidden and useful patterns in a text database [1, 2]. In addition, numerous works show that self-organizing maps (SOMs) [3] are effective in classifying a collection of text documents and building two-dimensional maps.
Previously, we proposed an approach for decision making of corporate strategy that uses self-organizing patent maps labeled by technical terms [4, 5] and the analytic hierarchy process (AHP) [6]. First, we extracted keywords by text mining to transform patent documents into feature vectors of the companies. Second, we

inputted the feature matrix of technical terms and company names into SOMs to create patent maps labeled by the technical terms. Then, we considered several corporate strategies utilizing the patent maps and made a decision with AHP.

In this paper, we consider several corporate strategies on R&D of new products using two kinds of patent maps labeled by technical terms and company names. We applied our approach to patent area of information home appliance and home network. We used 556 registered patents which were applied from 2000 to 2014 in Japan to show examples of creating self-organizing patent maps, considering corporate strategies and decision making with AHP.

2 Creating Self-Organizing Patent Maps

The SOM algorithm is based on unsupervised, competitive learning [3]. It provides a topology preserving mapping from the high dimensional space to map units. Map units, or neurons, usually form a two-dimensional lattice and thus the mapping is a mapping from high dimensional space onto a plane.

We collected 556 registered patent documents (in Japanese) containing summary and claims from the J-PlatPat (Japanese Platform of Patent Information) provided by Japan's National Center for Industrial Property Information and Training using the keywords "information home appliance" and "home network." The number of applicants was 85 from the time period 2000 to 2014. In order of the number of patents, the company names are C1 to C85.The number of registered patents of C1, C2 and C3 is 76, 56 and 47, respectively. We extract technical terms by word frequency analysis. We extract nouns whose frequency is five or more and whose number of letters is three or more. We ignore words which are vague, such as "computer," "data," or "system." We also extract technical terms by dependence relation analysis. Here, we extract nouns according to four cues of Japanese words: *hon-hatumei* (this invention), *teikyou* (offer), *kadai* (problem) and *mokuteki* (purpose) [7]. We extracted 27 words by using the word frequency and dependence relation analysis. We considered similar words as one word to reduce the number of words because a large number of words cannot be used to cluster patents using SOM. Table 1 shows part of the feature matrix. For example, the number of "Rooter" in all patents of C2 is eight.

Table 1. Part of the feature matrix.

(a) Part of the feature matrix for patent maps labeled by company names.

Company name	Rooter	Routing	Roaming
C1	1	1	1
C2	8	3	1
C3	1	2	2

(b) Part of the feature matrix for patent maps labeled by technical terms.

Technical term	C1	C2	C3
Rooter	1	8	1
Routing	1	3	2
Roaming	1	1	2

Figures 1, 2 and 3 show component maps of self-organizing patent map labeled by technical terms for C1, C2 and C3, respectively, in which a color scale shows the number of terms. Dark blue means that corresponding terms are not present. Red means that the frequency of occurrence of corresponding terms is high. As technical terms "Mobile," "Agent" and "Gateway" are located near, these terms are closely related. C2 is superior to C1 in agent and mobile technology. C3 is superior to C1 in gateway technology. C1 is superior to C2 and C3 in contents technology.

Figures 4 and 5 show component maps of self-organizing patent map labeled by company names for contents and audio-signal, respectively. As C3, C5, C7 and C8 are located in the same cluster, these companies are similar in patents on information home appliance. According to Figure 4, C5 has many patents on contents. According to Figure 5, only C2 has a patent on audio-signal.

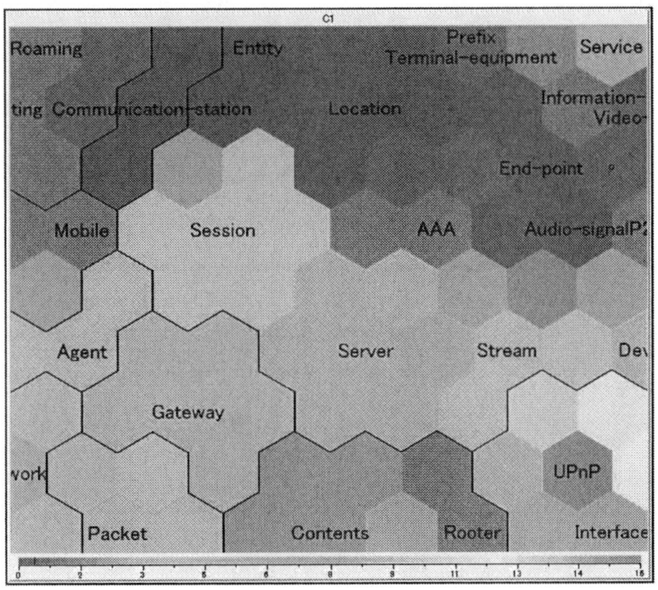

Fig. 1. Self-organizing patent map labeled by technical terms for C1.

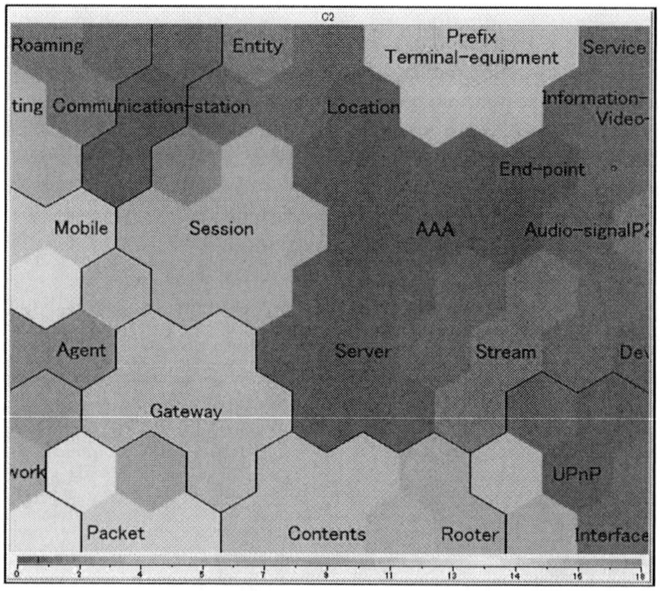

Fig. 2. Self-organizing patent map labeled by technical terms for C2.

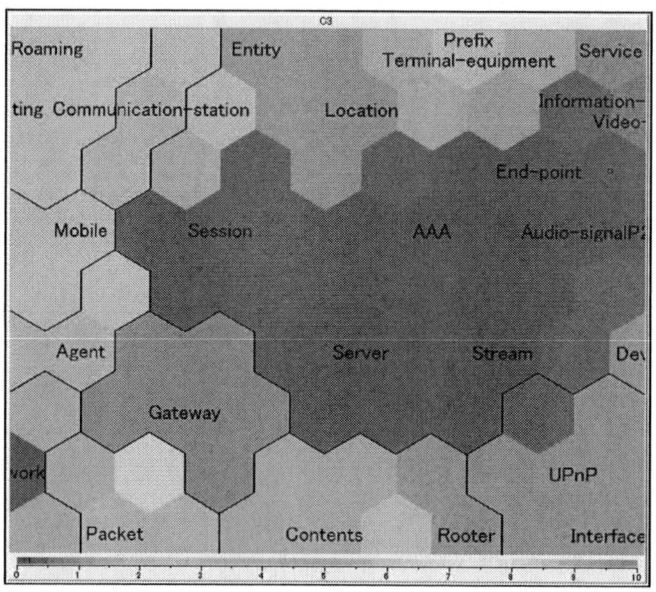

Fig. 3. Self-organizing patent map labeled by technical terms for C3.

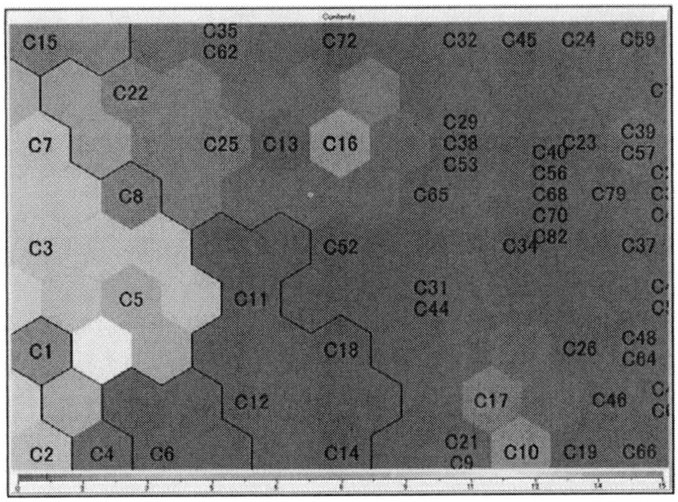

Fig. 4. Self-organizing patent map labeled by company names for contents.

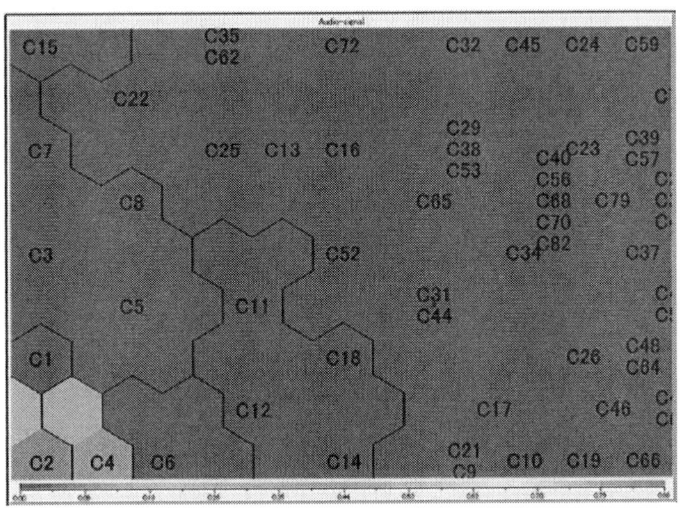

Fig. 5. Self-organizing patent map labeled by company names for audio-signal.

3 Considering Corporate Strategies

Here, we propose an improved way of considering corporate strategies with self-organizing patent maps labeled by technical terms (technical patent map) and company names (company patent map). Here, we consider corporate strategies of C2 who will overcome C1 in collaboration with C3 if necessary.

Step 1: Decide the target company for whom corporate strategies are considered. Here, we decided C2 who is one of leading companies in the field of information home appliance.

Step 2: Decide the company who is competitive with the company decided in Step 1. Here, we decided C1 whose number of registered patents on information home appliance is the most.

Step 3: Decide the company with whom the company decided in Step 1 is in collaboration if necessary. Here, we decided C3 who is also one of leading companies.

Step 4: Find technical terms which appear more frequently in the technical patent map of C2 or C3 than in the technical patent map of C1, by observing technical patent maps. Consider a corporate strategy in which C2 will promote product development using the technology as a selling point.

Step 5: Find technical terms which appear more frequently in the technical patent map of C1 than in the technical patent map of C2 and C3, by observing technical patent maps. Consider a corporate strategy in which C2 will promote research and development (R&D) on the technology, or find company X which has the technology, by observing company patent maps, and promote product development by working together with X.

Step 6: Find technical terms which don't appear in the technical patent map of C1, C2 and C3, by observing technical patent maps. Consider a corporate strategy in which C2 will promote R&D on the technology, or find other company Y which has the technology, by observing company patent maps, and promote product development by working together with Y.

Step 7: Find technical terms which only C2 or C3 has, by observing company patent maps, and promote product development using the technology as a selling point.

According to the above steps, we considered the following corporate strategy.

Strategy 1: C2 makes plans for business expansion using the C2's patent on a mobile device which has multiple interfaces. For example, C2 promotes development of the product which realizes remote control of home devices connected to home network using a mobile phone which has a mobile phone interface and a wireless LAN interface. This strategy is considered by **Step 4**.

Strategy 2: C2 makes plans for business expansion on wireless communication using the C2's patent on an agent technology plus the C2's and C3's patents on a home gateway technology. For example, C2 promotes development of the product which realizes switching the optimum route to the external network at high speed, setting home agent's home link automatically and properly, and sharing home devices connected to home network by multiple services. This is considered by **Step 4**.

Strategy 3: As C1 has patents on playing contents, C2 enters into licensing agreements with C5 who has patents on playing contents. For example, C2 promotes development of the product which realizes cooperate playing multiple contents with multiple recording and playback terminals connected to home network. This strategy is considered by **Step 5**.

Strategy 4: As C2 has a patent on audio equipment, C2 makes plans for business expansion using the C2's patent on audio signal. For example, C2 promotes development of the product which realizes receiving digital media such as music and movie files by connecting with any service providers using vehicle communication system equipped with audio equipment. This strategy is considered by **Step 7**.

4 Corporate Decision Making with AHP

AHP is a multi-criteria decision method that uses hierarchical structures to represent a problem [6]. Pairwise comparisons are based on forming a judgment between two particular elements rather than attempting to prioritize an entire list of elements. The AHP scales of pairwise comparisons are shown in Table 2.

Table 2. The AHP scales for pairwise comparisons.

Intensity of importance	Definition and explanation
1	Equal importance
3	Moderate importance
5	Essential or strong importance
7	Demonstrated importance
9	Extreme importance
2, 4, 6, 8	Intermediate values between the two adjacent judgments when compromise is needed.

Figure 6 shows an example of the relative measurement AHP model created for the task of corporate decision making by C2. Here, we used the following four criteria: required time, income, human resources, and R&D funds.

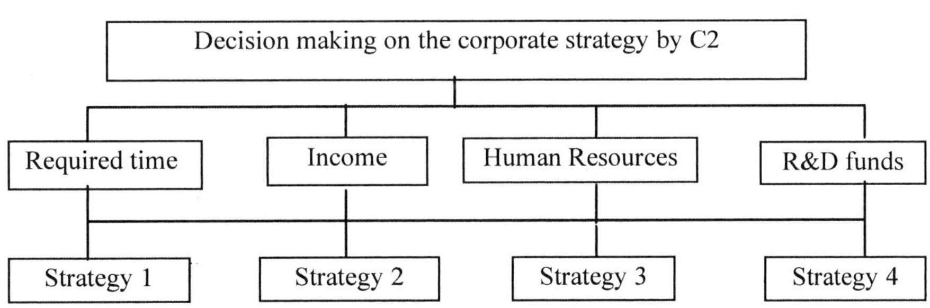

Figure 6: AHP model for corporate decision making by C2.

We assumed the pairwise comparison matrix for C2. The pairwise comparison matrix for the four criteria is shown in Table 3. Here, we assumed that required time is most important, income is second most important, and R&D funds are third most important. As a result, required time is most important and its weight is 0.468.

Table 3: Pairwise comparisons of four criteria.

	Required time	Income	R&D funds	Human resources	Weight
Required time	1	2	3	4	0.468
Income	1/2	1	2	3	0.277
R&D funds	1/3	1/2	1	2	0.160
Human resources	1/4	1/3	1/2	1	0.095

Consistency index = 0.01

Consistency index shows whether the pairwise comparison is appropriate or not. When the index is lower than 0.1, the pairwise comparison is appropriate. When the index is over 0.1, the comparison is not appropriate and should be corrected. In this case, consistency index was 0.01 and the pairwise comparison was appropriate.

The pairwise comparisons of four alternatives with respect to required time are shown in Table 4. The weights of Strategies 1 and 4 were highest. Because C2 makes plans for business expansion using his own technology in Strategies 1 and 4, we assumed that the required time of Strategies 1 and 4 is shortest.

Table 4: Pairwise comparisons of alternatives with respect to required time.

	Strategy 1	Strategy 2	Strategy 3	Strategy 4	Weight
Strategy 1	1	3	3	1	0.375
Strategy 2	1/3	1	1	1/3	0.125
Strategy 3	1/3	1	1	1/3	0.125
Strategy 4	1	3	3	1	0.375

Consistency index = 0

The pairwise comparisons of four alternatives with respect to income are shown in Table 5. The weights of Strategies 1 and 2 were highest. Because we assumed that Strategies 1 and 2 are related to key technology of information home appliance and are most profitable.

Table 5: Pairwise comparisons of alternatives with respect to income.

	Strategy 1	Strategy 2	Strategy 3	Strategy 4	Weight
Strategy 1	1	1	3	5	0.390
Strategy 2	1	1	3	5	0.390
Strategy 3	1/3	1/3	1	3	0.152
Strategy 4	1/5	1/5	1/3	1	0.068

Consistency index = 0.015

The pairwise comparisons of four alternatives with respect to human resources are shown in Table 6. The weight of Strategy 2 was highest, because the number of inventors of C2 and C3 on Strategy 2 is the largest.

Table 6: Pairwise comparisons of alternatives with respect to human resources.

	Strategy 1	Strategy 2	Strategy 3	Strategy 4	Weight
Strategy 1	1	1/3	3	1	0.200
Strategy 2	3	1	5	3	0.522
Strategy 3	1/3	1/5	1	1/3	0.078
Strategy 4	1	1/3	3	1	0.200

Consistency index = 0.014

The pairwise comparisons of four alternatives with respect to R&D funds are shown in Table 7. The weights of Strategies 1, 2 and 4 were highest, because there are patents of C2 and C3 in these strategies.

Table 7: Pairwise comparisons of alternatives with respect to R&D funds.

	Strategy 1	Strategy 2	Strategy 3	Strategy 4	Weight
Strategy 1	1	1	3	1	0.300
Strategy 2	1	1	3	1	0.300
Strategy 3	1/3	1/3	1	1/3	0.100
Strategy 4	1	1	3	1	0.300

Consistency index = 0

Table 8 shows final results of AHP. Strategy 1 (mobile device) was the best. Because we assumed that short required time is most important and high income is second most important. The required time of Strategy 1 is shortest and the income of Strategy 1 is highest. Strategy 1 is selected as the final choice.

Table 8: Final results of AHP.

Criteria	Required time	Income	R&D funds	Human resources	Result
Weight of criteria	0.468	0.277	0.160	0.095	
Strategy 1	0.375	0.390	0.300	0.200	0.351
Strategy 2	0.125	0.390	0.300	0.522	0.264
Strategy 3	0.125	0.152	0.100	0.078	0.124
Strategy 4	0.375	0.068	0.300	0.200	0.261

5 Conclusion

We proposed an improved way of considering corporate strategies with self-organizing patent maps labeled by technical terms and company names. Then, we applied our approach to patent area of information home appliance to show examples of considering corporate strategies and decision making with AHP. We are sorry that we don't explain details because of limited pages (ten pages). In future work, we will apply our way to the other patent area. We will use other types of AHP [6] and ANP [8] for decision making.

References

1. Yoon, B., Yoon, C., Park, Y.: On the development and application of a self-organizing feature map-based patent map. R&D Management, vo. 4, pp. 291-300 (2002)
2. Jun, S.: Technology marketing using PCA, SOM, and STP strategy modelling. IJCSI International Journal of Computer Science Issues, vol. 8, no.1, pp.87-92 (2011)
3. Kohonen, T.: Self-Organizing Maps. Springer, New York (1995)
4. Kohara, K., Kato, T., Kouno, H.: Corporate Decision Making with Self-Organizing Patent Maps Labelled by Technical Terms and AHP. Proc. of Conf-IRM 2012, Paper 21 (2012)
5. Kohara, K., Maeda, Y.: Considering Corporate Strategies with Self-Organizing Patent Maps and Decision Making with AHP. Proc. of Conf-IRM 2015, Paper 39 (2015)
6. Saaty, T.: The Analytic Hierarchy Process. McGraw-Hill, New York (1980)
7. Sakai, H., Nonaka, H., Masuyama, S.: Extraction of information on the purpose and the technical effect from a patent document. The 23rd Annual Conference of the Japanese Society for Artificial Intelligence. (in Japanese) (2009)
8. Saaty, T.: The Analytic Network Process. Expert Choice, Arlington (1996)

Particle Filter in Single Object Tracking with MapReduce

Di Wang and Min Chen

State University of New York at New Paltz,
1 Hawk Drive, New Paltz, NY, USA
{wangd4, chenm@newpaltz.edu}

Abstract: Particle filter is one of the techniques which has been widely used in object tracking. Due to the virtue of extendability and flexibility on both linear and non-linear environments, various particle filter based trackers have been proposed in the literature. However, the conventional approach cannot handle very large videos efficiently in the current data intensive information age. In this work, a parallelized particle filter is provided in a distributed framework provided by the Hadoop/Map-Reduce infrastructure to tackle object tracking tasks. The experiments indicate that the proposed algorithm has a better convergence and accuracy as compared to the traditional particle filter. The computational power and the scalability of the proposed particle filter in single object tracking have been enhanced as well.

Keywords: MapReduce, Particle Filter, Single Object Tracking.

1 Introduction

Object tracking is a challenging task in many computer vision applications including surveillance, gesture recognition, vehicle tracking, medical imaging, etc [1]. Object tracking aims to identify the target state using trajectory, orientation, position and scale within a sequence of video. In particular, the tracking agent estimates the moving object frame by frame and labels the area of interest in the video frame based on the previous state [2]. The challenges of object tracking arise due to the noise in images, the complexity of object movements, the illumination of changing scenes and the difficulty of defining object shapes. In order to simplify the task, most approaches make the assumption that no abrupt changes between the object movements. In addition, the object is moving in a constant velocity with an acceleration based on the previous knowledge.

In light of the difference of object representation, image feature, model of motion, appearance and shape of object [3], a variety of tracking algorithms have been proposed in object tracking. Generally, there are two categories: deterministic approaches and stochastic approaches. Deterministic approaches typically use an iterative search to track the local optima with a cost function. The cost function measures the similarity between the current image and the template image. On the other hand, stochastic approaches model the underlying dynamics of the tracking system using state space. There is exactly one mode in the posterior probability density function (pdf) in a linear-Gaussian model with linear measurement [4]. Kalman filter is one popular method to propagate and update the mean and covariance of the the distribution. However, it is impossible to estimate the distribution analytically in nonlinear or non-Gaussian problem. Sequential Monte Carlo, also known as particle filter, is a widely used approach which recursively constructs the pdf of the state space using Monte Carlo integration [5].

Particle filter is easy to extend and it provides the flexibility to handle both non-linear and non-normal object models. Contours, color features and appearance model are commonly used in the particle filter approach [6]. Particle filter approximates the filtered pdf by a set of weighted particles in any state model. The likelihood score is used to measure the weighted particles. Tremendous amount of videos from all applications have been accumulated, how to analyze these videos efficiently and on time is challenging. However, most of the particle filter-based algorithms have paid little attention on how to parallelize the framework in order to handle the large volume of videos in a reasonable time. Recently, MapReduce framework has gained significant momentum from industry and academic because of its simplicity, scalability and fault tolerance. This programming paradigm is a scalable and fault-tolerant data processing tool that was developed to provide significant improvements in large-scale data-intensive applications in clusters. Based on the aforementioned reasons, a parallel particle filter is conducted in a distributed framework provided by the Hadoop/Map-Reduce infrastructure in this work. We aims to propose particle filter with Hadoop/MapReduce to enhance the computational power and the scalability of parallel particle filter in single-object tracking.

The rest of the paper is organized as follows: the proposed MapReduce based algorithm is demonstrated in Section 2. The experimental results and analysis are described in Section 3, and the paper is concluded in Section 4.

2 Approach

2.1 Particle Filter

Particle filter is one of Bayesian sequential importance sampling techniques. A finite set of weighted samples is used to recursively approximate the posterior distribution. Prediction and update are two essential steps in particle filter. Given all the observations up to time $t-1$, denotes as $z_{1:t-1} = z_1, .., z_{t-1}$, the probabilistic system transition model $p(x_t|x_{t-1})$ is used in the prediction stage to predict the posterior at time t:

$$p(x_t|z_{1:t-1}) = \int p(x_t|x_{t-1})p(x_{t-1}|z_{1:t-1})dx_{t-1} \quad (1)$$

The state at time t with an obersavation z_t is updated using Bayes' rule:

$$p(x_t|z_{1:t}) = \frac{p(z_t|x_t)p(x_t|z_{1:t-1})}{p(z_t|z_{1:t-1})} \quad (2)$$

where $p(z_t|x_t)$ is described by the observation equation. A finite set of N samples $X_t = x_t^1,\ldots,x_t^N$ with importance weight $W_t = w_t^1,\ldots,w_t^N$ is used to recursively approximate the posterior in Eq.2. The weight of each sample is calculated as:

$$w_t^i = w_{t-1}^i \frac{p(z_t|x_t^i)p(x_t^i|x_{t-1}^i)}{p(x_t|x_{1:t-1},z_{1:t})} \quad (3)$$

In order to avoid degeneracy, the importance weights are used to resample the samples and an unweighted particle set is generated. The procedure of proposed particle filter for single object tracking is listed in Algorithm 1.

Algorithm 1: Particle Filter for Single Object Tracking

procedure Main;
initialization;
initial particle location matrix P_1
foreach $i \in P_1$ **do**
  $i \leftarrow random$(height,width)
end
procedure Map;
Input : a set of consecutive frame X, a set of particle locations P_i, $i \in \{2,\ldots,n\}$ and Interference parameters: p, v and c
Output: new sets of particles P_i' and a new set of detected frame X'
for $i \leftarrow 2$ ***to*** P_n **do**
  $P_i \leftarrow updateParticles(P_{i-1}, p, v)$;
  for $j \leftarrow 1$ ***to*** P_i **do**
    $C_j \leftarrow getRGB(P_i)$;
    $W_i \leftarrow calWeight(C_j, c)$;
  end
  $Pi \leftarrow resampling(W, P_i)$;
  $X'i \leftarrow drawParticles(X_i, P_i)$;
end

2.2 Hadoop Video Processing Interface

Hadoop Video Processing Interface (HVPI) [7] is a video processing interface which can be used over the Hadoop infrastructure. It is an open-source application that allows video analytic applications to work in the Hadoop infrastructure. Most of existing video analytic applications are implemented by C/C++ such as OpenCV but they are not compatible with Hadoop. Apache Hadoop is a widely deployed distributed storage to process big data. However, programming framework like MapReduce using Hadoop has limited supports for the mainstream video analytic applications.

One of the solution is the use of Java Native Interface (JNI) [8] which integrates a Java application with legacy code written in languages such as C/C++ [9]. Though it enables native code to run on the Hadoop infrastructue, the code complexity arises. It is hard for configuration if some incompatible issues happen. Another solution is the use of streaming API of Hadoop to encapsulate any scripting language. HVPI adopted this way to provide an easy-to-use video r/w interface for users to quickly build large-scale video analytic applications based on Hadoop and the user can easily migrate the existing video analytic applications written in other programming languages into Hadoop platform [7].

2.3 Proposed Approach

Single-frame oriented video analytic approach and frame-series oriented video analytic approach are two typical strategies for video processing [10]. The single-frame oriented video analytic approach processes each single frame without any association. On the other hand, frame-series oriented video analytic approach is different which processes a certain number of correlated frames at the same time. The HVPI takes the advantages of both to provide an interface in a distributed environment. The MapReduce framework splits a video sequence into independent chunks which processes frame by frame in a parallel manner. These procedures are illustrated in the Fig. 1.

This framework demonstrates the map step for the proposed algorithm. The proposed algorithm starts with the preparation of particles and the selection of background image. Each map step reads a single frame of the input video. The selective background image is used for background subtraction. The proposed algorithm 2.1 is then applied to object tracking. In order to see the distribution of the particles, the particles are drawn in the original image and the results are emitted to the reduce step as well. The reduce step computes the results and save them in the HDFS as designed. The map function and reduce function are illustrated in Algorithm 2.

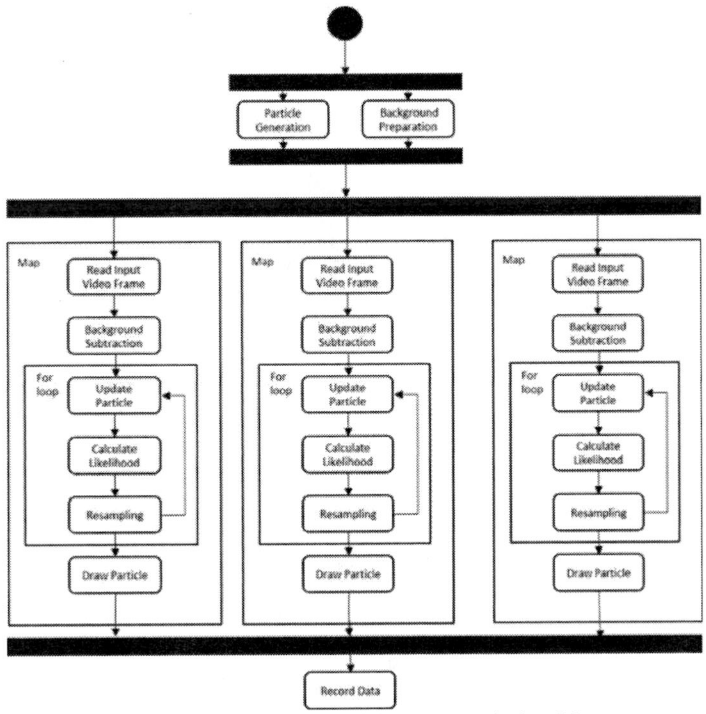

Figure 1: A framework of the proposed algorithm.

Algorithm 2: HVPI algorithm for Single Object Tracking

procedure Map $(key, value)$;
Input : Frame ID Strings key and its attributes $value$
Output: Frame ID Strings key and particles p
$image \leftarrow value$
$background \leftarrow 1st frame$
Using Background Subtraction to remove the background in $image$
Updating each particle from particles p
Calculating likelihood of particles p on the object
$resampling \quad p \leftarrow resampling(p, likelihood)$
Drawing particles p on $image$
emit(key, p)
procedure Reducer $(key, \mathcal{P})$;
Input : Frame ID Strings key and a list of particles p from each frames
Output: Particles p in each frames and its noise
foreach $v \in \mathcal{P}$ **do**
| result.add(v)
end
emit(result)

3 Experiments and Results

3.1 Environmental Setup

The experiments are conducted on an Apache Hadoop cluster with two data nodes using MapReduce. The two data nodes are setting in a virtual machine using VMware workstation pro 12.5 on a Windows machine (Intel(R) Core(TM) i7-6700K CPU 4.00GHz 4.01GHz). The video set is adopted from [14] and [15]. The first video has a lady in red walks in and out a room. The second video is a person in gray walking in the hallway of a shopping mall.

3.2 Background Subtraction

In order to detect a dynamic object from a video sequence, the background subtraction is a popular technique which is used for foreground segmentation by comparing current frame with the background image. The background images need to be preprocessed by image binarization [11]. An adaptive threshold is applied to binarize the images. The threshold is calculated by Otsuâ€™s method which is used to reduce the gray-level of image to a binary image [12].

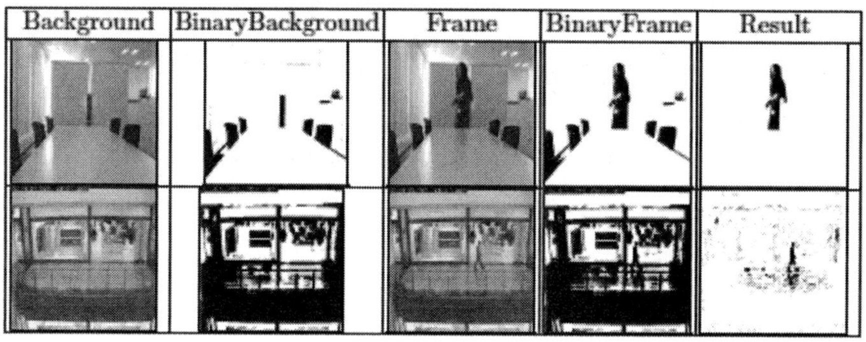

Fig. 2: Background subtraction.

In Fig. 1, the background images are listed in the first column. The second column is the binary images after image binarization. The third column includes the sample frames in the two videos. The fourth column lists the binary images and the background substraction results are demonstrated in the last column.

3.3 Tracking Results

In order to evaluate the tracking result, the proposed PF with MapReduce (MPF) is compared with the conventional particle filter (PF) using 800 and 1600 particles, respectively in Fig. 2. The PF calculates the color likelihood which is tracking the red color of the person. However, the proposed MFP can track the person video with better accuracy and it's not limited to red color. Moreover, the MPF can converge much faster than CPF.

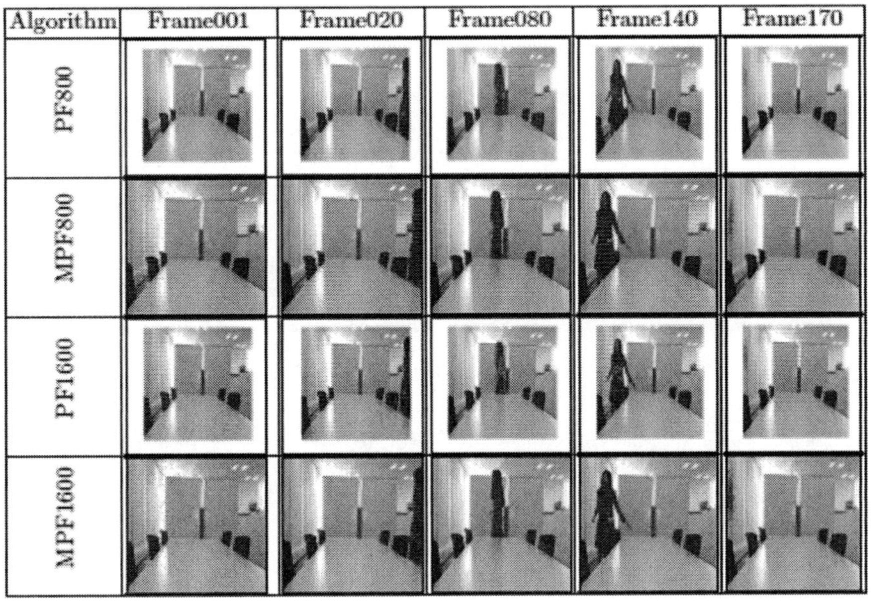

Fig. 3: A comparison of conventional particle filter (CPF) and particle filter with MapReduce (MPF) using 800 and 1600 particles, respectively.

Furthermore, the tracking result of the proposed MPF applied to a shopping mall video using 800 particles is listed in Fig. 3. The result of 1600 particles is also illustrated in Fig. 4. The results indicate that a large number of particles can converge much faster and provide better accuracy as compared to a smaller number of particles.

3.4 Execution Time

Another important performance measurement for object tracking is the execution time. In Fig. 3, the execution time of the proposed algorithm is estimated on a single-node Hadoop cluster and a two-node clusters. The experiment is conducted with the number of particles varying from 800 to 12800. The proposed algorithm can process 12 frames per second in a single-node machine. It then increases to 13 frames per second for two-node cluster. The overall performance indicates that two-node cluster is faster than the single-node cluster.

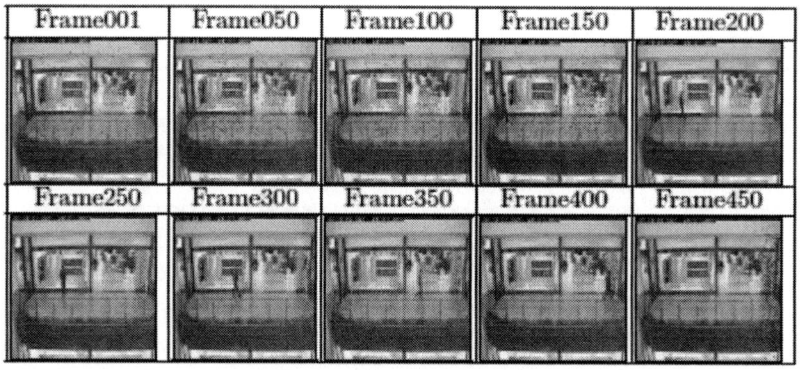

Fig. 4: A list of frames using MPF with 800 particles.

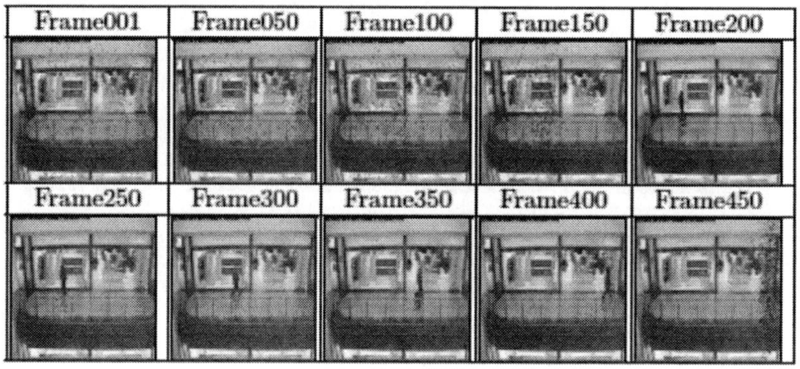

Fig. 5: A list of frames using MPF with 1600 particles.

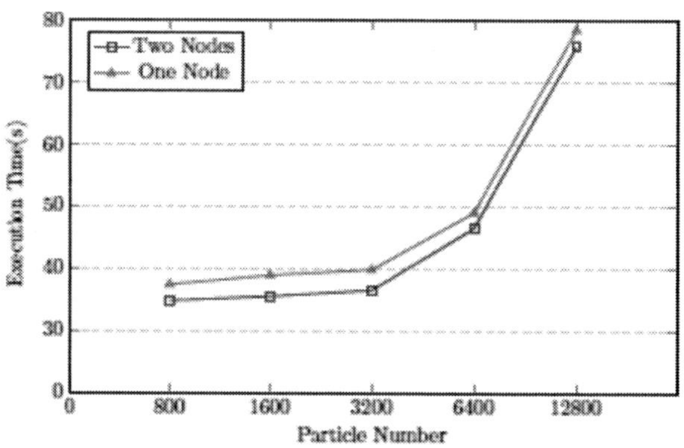

Fig. 6: Execution time comparison.

4 Conclusion

A parallelized particle filter has been proposed to overcome the problems identified by previous approaches, where the MapReduce mechanism is used to explore the scalability. Experiments and results demonstrated that the proposed method (MPF) does improve the tracking performance without introducing extra computational cost. The proposed algorithm will be improved to do multiple-object tracking and some other edge detection techniques can be adopted to improve the performance of the proposed MPF.

References

1. A. Yilmaz, O. Javed, M. Shah. Object tracking: A survey. ACM Comput. Surv. 38, 4, Article 13, 45 pages, 2006.
2. A. Dick, A. V. D. Hengel, C. Shen, W. Hu, X. Li, Z. Zhang,. A survey of appearance models in visual object tracking. ACM transactions on Intelligent Systems and Technology (TIST), 4(4), 58, 2013.
3. G. Xia, and S. A. Ludwig. "Object-tracking based on particle filter using particle swarm optimization with density estimation." Evolutionary Computation (CEC), 2016 IEEE Congress on. IEEE, 2016.
4. C. Yang, L. Davis and R. Duraiswami,. "Fast multiple object tracking via a hierarchical particle filter." Computer Vision, 2005. ICCV 2005. Tenth IEEE International Conference on. Vol. 1. IEEE, 2005.
5. A. Doucet, N. de Freitas, and N. Gordon, editors. Sequential Monte Carlo Methods in Practice. Springer-Verlag, New York, 2001.
6. A. D. Jepson, D. J. Fleet, and T. F. El-Maraghi. Robust online appearance models for visual tracking. IEEE Trans. Pattern Anal. Mach. Intell., 25(10):12961311, Oct. 2003.
7. H. Ma, H. Tang, H. Zhang, X. Zhao, and Y. Kou,. HVPI: extending Hadoop to support video analytic applications. In Cloud Computing (CLOUD), 2015 IEEE 8th International Conference on (pp. 789-796). IEEE 2015.
8. R. Gordon, Essential JNI: Java Native Interface. PrenticeHall, Inc., 1998.
9. S. Liang. The Java Native Interface: Programmer's Guide and Specification. Addison-Wesley Professional, 1999.
10. H. L. Tan and L. D. Chen, An approach for fast and parallel video processing on apache hadoop clusters.
11. D. M. Tsai and S. C. Lai, "Independent component analysis-based background subtraction for indoor surveillance." IEEE Transactions on Image Processing 18.1 (2009): 158-167.
12. M. Sezgin & B. Sankur (2004). "Survey over image thresholding techniques and quantitative performance evaluation". Journal of Electronic Imaging. 13 (1): 146165.
13. K. Li, S. A. Ludwig and M. Chen, Clustering in Big Data, Big Data: Management, Architecture, and Processing, (2017) 333-346.
14. MathWorks(2016), Image Acquisition Toolbox: MATLAB 7.13 (R2011b).
15. EC Funded CAVIAR project, EC Funded CAVIAR project/IST 2001 37540 `http://homepages.inf .ed.ac.uk/rbf/CAVIAR/`.

Edge Detection Using MapReduce Based Ant Colony Optimization

Michael J. Papesca and Min Chen

State University of New York at New Paltz, 1 Hawk Drive, New Paltz, NY, USA
michael.papesca@gmail.com chenm@newpaltz.edu

Abstract. The need to understand and handle large and complex image data is critical in many fields in the current information age. Edge detection, a common technique used in image processing, uses discontinuities in image properties to identify boundaries of objects in images. It is a basic tool in machine vision and computer vision, particularly for automatic feature detection and feature extraction. However, traditional edge detection approaches cannot detect edges in images in a timely manner due to memory and computational time constraints. In this work, we propose a novel parallelized ant colony optimization technique in a distributed framework provided by the Hadoop/Map-Reduce infrastructure to improve the edge detection capabilities. Moreover, a filtering technique is applied to reduce the noisy background of images to achieve significant improvement in the accuracy of edge detection. We also study the scalability and effectiveness of the proposed algorithm.

Keywords: Edge Detection, Ant Colony Optimization and MapReduce.

1 Introduction

Edge detection is one of the most frequently used techniques in computer vision since the early 1970s [1]. Edge detection is a fundamental preprocessing step for a variety of application, including object tracking [2], segmentation [4], and active contours [3]. The image edges are detected and grouped into contours or surfaces to represent the boundaries of the objects. Edge detection aims to segment an image by finding and placing sharp discontinuities in gray level images. Many edge detection techniques have been reported in previous works such as Canny [5], Sobel [6], Prewitt [7], Log [8] etc. However, without optimization techniques, most of the existing detection techniques use a huge search space [9] for the image edge detection. Hence, the edge detection task consumes considerable memory and time.

Ant colony optimization (ACO) [10] is an evolutionary computation-based algorithm inspired by the natural phenomenon of ants' foraging. In this optimization method, ants follow an intelligent way of information transfer about the food sources to the rest of the colony with the help of some natural chemical secretion (pheromone) [9]. The deposited pheromone slowly evaporates over time while the ants are walking to and from the food source. Other ants observe the presence of pheromone trails and follow paths with highest concentration of pheromone. The shortest path receives the greatest pheromone concentration as more ants travel over it. Thus, the ants eventually will travel the shorter path with this positive feedback mechanism. Several techniques have been proposed to handle the edge detection using ACO. In [9] proposed an ACO edge detection using F ratio-based technique. An ant colony optimization based mechanism to compensate broken edges was presented in citeLu. It adopted four moving policies to reduce the computation load. An ACO-based edge detection approach was introduced in [12] to tackle the image edge detection problem. All these approaches indicate that ACO is a promising technique for edge detection.

However, because of the sheer volume and increasing complexity of image data being collected and created in the field of computer vision, the aforementioned approaches are inadequate to handle very large image data in a timely manner. In order to process this big data, both increased computer performance and improved algorithms that allow the exploration of large parameter spaces are necessary. MapReduce [13] is one of the most efficient big data solutions, which enables the processing of a massive volume of data in parallel with many low-end computing nodes. This programming paradigm is a scalable and fault-tolerant data processing tool that was developed to provide significant improvements in large-scale data-intensive applications in clusters.

This work proposes a novel algorithm in the field of edge detection in images using a MapReduce based ant colony optimization (ACO) with filtering, to extract edge information from the pheromone matrix. The proposed algorithm takes advantage of both ACO and parallel computing. We test the algorithm on a greyscale image set, a colored-greyscale image set and a color image set. The experimental results show that both statistically and visually this method performs better than the earlier reported techniques.

The rest of the paper is organized as follows: the proposed algorithm is demonstrated in Section 2. The experimental results and analysis are described in Section 3, and Section 4 concludes the paper.

2 Proposed Approach

The proposed approach has three major steps: preprocessing step, map step and reduce step.

2.1 Preprocessing Step

The proposed algorithm starts with a preprocessing step. The images need to be preprocessed in order to convert them to computable formats which the map step can process. The images are converting into an image matrix pixel by pixel.

2.2 Map Step

The next step of the proposed algorithm is the map step. This is the crucial part of the algorithm. Each preprocessed image matrix is the input of the map step. The image is segmented with a grid of 5-pixel × 5-pixel, 10-pixel × 10-pixel, 15pixel × 15-pixel, 20-pixel × 20-pixel, and 25-pixel × 25-pixel, respectively. The ant colony algorithm uses the segmentation results to detect the images edges. The edges are emitted as the output of the map step. The detail explanation is listed in Algorithm 1.

Algorithm 1 Map Function.

```
Input: Image pixel data
Output: Key-value pairs for pixel pheromones
procedure MAPPER(input_data)
    for each line of input_data do
        Split line into components
        for range 0 to segment size as y do
            for range 0 to segment size as x do
                Image_matrix[x, y] = component
                Increment to next component from input_data line
            end for
        end for
    end for
    Process edge of image in image_matrix        ▷ The input_data is from the image
    for rows in edge as row do
        for pixels in row as pixel do
            print data from pixel
        end for
    end for
end procedure
```

Edge Detection with ACO: The proposed edge detection with ACO starts with the initialization of ants. It then runs iteratively to construct and update the pheromone matrix. To perform edge detection with ACO, two major functions need to be redesigned. First is how to determine the moving direction of each ant. Multiple observable conditions present at the time of movement along with a component of random chance need to be considered in a weighted approach. Eq. 1 is calculated to decide the moving direction of each ant.

$$w_{ij} = P[i, j]^{\alpha} + I[i, j]^{\beta} \tag{1}$$

where w_{ij} represents the neighboring pixel at location (i, j). P [i, j] represents the current pheromone level at the pixel with the pheromone matrix P . I[i, j] represents the pixel value of the original image. α and β represent the weights given to the pheromone level and pixel values respectively within this equation.

Another function to consider is the pheromone deposit. The equation that determines the pheromone drop quantity is (see Eq. 2).

$$d = \frac{|I[i, j] - I[x, y]|}{\lambda} \tag{2}$$

λ where d represents the pheromone drop amount after each ant step. I is the same as before. λ is the scaling factor of the pheromone deposit. Once all steps are completed, the pheromone matrix P gets filled with different levels of pheromone at each pixel. To reduce the amount of excess edge data that could be caused by lower amount of pheromones, a filter method is adopted to select the cutoff level (see Algorithm 2). The detailed procedures are listed in Algorithm 3. The final edge results are produced for the following reduce step.

Algorithm 2 Filtering pheromone drop amounts.

```
Input: Current and previous pixels
Output: Pheromone drop quantity
procedure FILTER(previous_pixel, current_pixel)
    if percent-difference(previous_pixel, current_pixel) < limit then
        Drop no pheromones
    else
        Follow normal pheromone drop equation
    end if
end procedure
```

2.3 Reduce Step

The majority of processing is done in the mapper function. The main purpose of the reducer step is to condense the data back together. The output of detection results are stored in the HDFS as designed.

Algorithm 3 Edge detection with ACO.

```
Input: Image
Output: The resulting edge
procedure FINDEDGES(image)
    Convert image to pixel data
    Create matrix of pixel data
    Initialize matrix of ants
    for all steps do
        for all ants do
            Calculate next step probabilities
            Choose direction to move in
            Deposit pheromones
        end for
        Simulate pheromone evaporation
    end for
    Calculate good pheromone level cutoff
    Filter good and bad pheromone edge data
    Create Edge from good pheromone edge data
end procedure
```

3 Experiments and Results

3.1 Environmental Setup

The experiments are conducted both on a single-node Windows machine (Intel Core i7-7500U Kaby Lake (2.7 GHz, up to 3.5 GHz, 4 MB cache, 2 cores)) and m3.xlarge EC2 instances (Intel Xeon Processor E5-2670 v2 Ivy Bridge (2.50 GHz, 25MB Cache, 4 cores)) from AWS. The parameters values are listed in Tabel 1. 30 images [14] which can be categorized into greyscale, colored-greyscale and color are used for experimental purpose.

Table 1: Parameters and values used in the proposed algorithm.

Parameter	Value
α	0.1
β	10
ϕ	0.5
λ	10
ρ	0.22

3.2 Experimental Results with ACO

Detection results with the selective images of the proposed mapreduce based unfiltered ACO and the filtered ACO are illustrated in Fig. 1. As shown in the figure, the segmentation steps are 5, 10, 15, 20 and 25 respectively. The first image is a sample for the greyscale image set. The filtered edge contains less background noise as compared to the unfiltered edges on all segmentation steps. The second image is a sample of colored-greyscale image set. Similarly, it has less noise on the background and the shadows around the content of the image have been mostly removed as well. The third image is a sample of color image set. It is clear that the background noise has been removed as compared to the unfiltered approach.

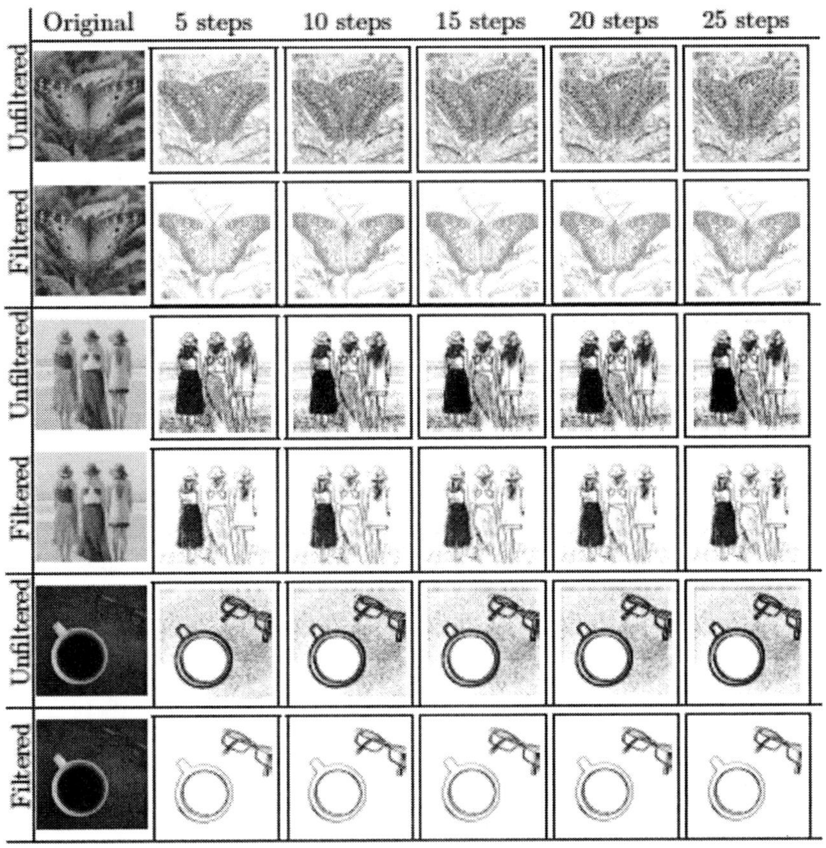

Fig. 1: Detection results using unfiltered ACO and filtered ACO.

3.3 Statistical Analysis

Mean Squared Error (MSE) and Peak Signal-to-Noise Ratio(PSNR) are used to compare the performance of the unfiltered ACO and the filtered ACO. The result with the 25 segmentation steps of the whole image sets is listed in Table 2.

Table 2: 25 step MSE & PSNR results.

	MSE		PSNR (dB)	
Image	Unfiltered	Filtered	Unfiltered	Filtered
bw_0_photo	21812.67	12919.88	4.74	7.02
bw_1_photo	33893.78	33363.99	2.83	2.90
bw_2_photo	28062.45	25991.47	3.65	3.98
bw_3_photo	32491.88	29575.38	3.01	3.42
bw_4_photo	39084.19	36740.86	2.21	2.48
bw_5_photo	22626.25	20167.21	4.58	5.08
bw_6_photo	34562.89	33989.78	2.74	2.82
bw_7_photo	28543.41	28417.90	3.58	3.59
bw_8_photo	24946.44	22346.87	4.16	4.64
bw_9_photo	24671.18	24325.25	4.21	4.27
colorbw_0_photo	30426.81	19747.05	3.30	5.18
colorbw_1_photo	33758.44	25942.12	2.85	3.99
colorbw_2_photo	32412.48	29974.06	3.02	3.36
colorbw_3_photo	32401.84	27957.81	3.03	3.67
colorbw_4_photo	47706.23	32408.86	1.35	3.02
colorbw_5_photo	26925.79	19558.21	3.83	5.22
colorbw_6_photo	45548.78	32258.15	1.55	3.04
colorbw_7_photo	27026.62	22210.96	3.81	4.67
colorbw_8_photo	52810.80	43495.22	0.90	1.75
colorbw_9_photo	19120.70	14257.94	5.32	6.59
color_0_photo	13707.68	10045.32	6.76	8.11
color_1_photo	28108.88	20801.43	3.64	4.95
color_2_photo	21972.93	12286.83	4.71	7.24
color_3_photo	16639.16	9879.53	5.92	8.18
color_4_photo	27000.44	16362.95	3.82	5.99
color_5_photo	11176.32	6173.68	7.65	10.23
color_6_photo	21781.89	15370.74	4.75	6.26
color_7_photo	20377.79	12744.96	5.04	7.08
color_8_photo	23624.78	14324.68	4.40	6.57
color_9_photo	42422.04	41814.26	1.85	-2.43

The result indicates that the filtered ACO consistently performances better as compared to the unfiltered ACO in terms of MSE and PSNR. Moreover, the unpaired t-test with a significance level of 0.5 is performed on the data set of the wo approaches.

The null hypothesis is applied (YOU SHOULD EXPLICITLY STATE THE NULL HYPOTHESIS, I THINK). The P-values produced in Table 3 show a very promising value to conclude that the improvements of the filtered edges over the unfiltered edges is not merely coincidental.

Table 3: T-test results.

Steps	T-Value	P-Value
5	-2.280	0.0262
10	-2.309	0.0244
15	-2.348	0.0222
20	-2.386	0.0202
25	-2.427	0.0183

3.4 Detection and Scalability Results using EMR

The filtered ACO was later implemented and run on the Amazon web service to explore its scalability. The detection results of the selective images are listed in Fig. 2. The results are consist with the experiments conducted on a single-node cluster. The filtered ACO performs better than the unfiltered ACO in terms of background noise. Later, we conduct a scalability analysis whereby the segmentation step is increased by 5 dimensions for the whole image set. We observe a normal linear trend of the execution time for increasing segmentation step given that the date set is fixed in Fig. 3. The last experiment conducts a scalability analysis whereby the number of data nodes are increased linearly with the same image set. A fixed segmentation step with value 10 is selected. The result is illustrated in Fig. 4. The execution time of the proposed algorithm follows a linear trend with the data node range from 2 to 16. However, it doesn't perform linearly when the data node reaches 16 due to the throughput.

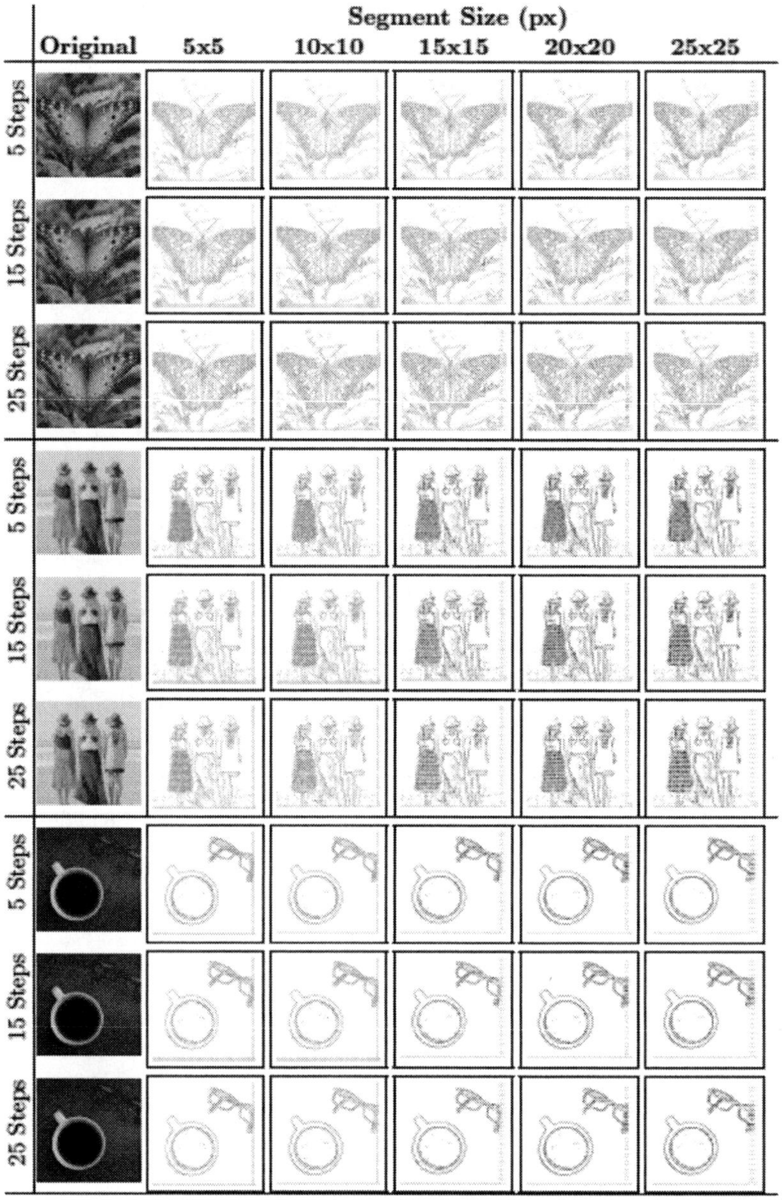

Fig. 2: Greyscale AWS Edges.

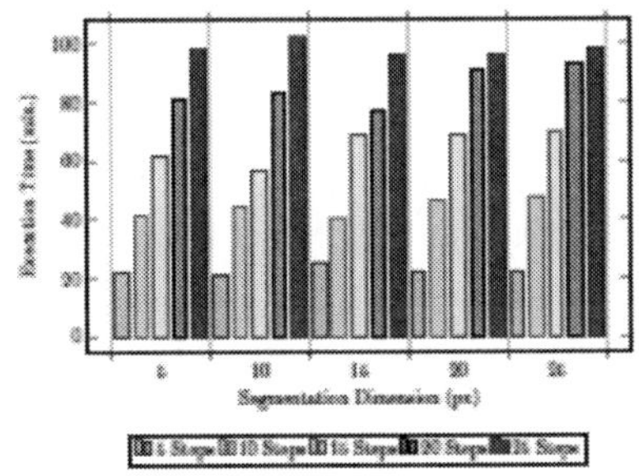

Fig. 3: Scalability of the proposed algorithm on EMR with 2 data nodes.

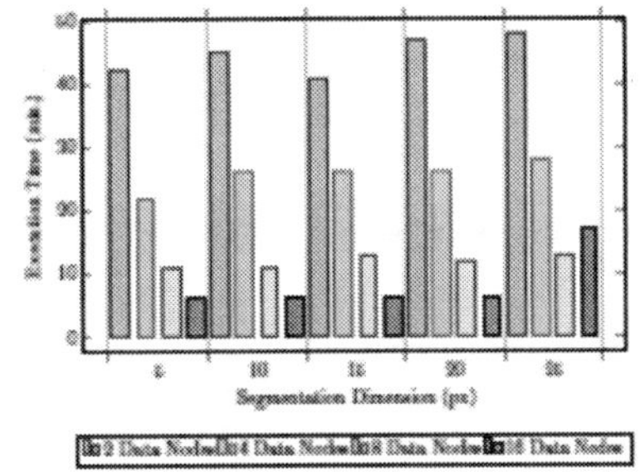

Fig. 4: Scalability of the proposed ACO with a segmentation step of 10.

4 Conclusion

In this paper, a novel ACO image edge detection with Hadoop MapReduce was successfully developed. The proposed method takes advantage of the parallelism of ACO, its rapid convergence, and the virtue of the MapReduce paradigm. As shown in Section 3 the results demonstrate the effectiveness of applying ACO edge detection algorithm on the distributed system like Hadoop MapReduce. In the future, we propose to apply the algorithm in an image processing pipeline for object recognition and object tracking with improved speed and accuracy.

References

1. N. Senthilkumaran, R. Rajesh, Edge detection techniques for image segmentation a survey of soft computing approaches, International journal of recent trends in engineering, 1(2),(2009).
2. Yilmaz, Alper, Omar Javed, and Mubarak Shah. Object tracking: A survey. Acm computing surveys (CSUR) 38.4 (2006): 13.
3. Chan, Tony F., and Luminita A. Vese. Active contours without edges. IEEE Transactions on image processing 10.2 (2001): 266-277.
4. Chen, Min, and Simone A. Ludwig. Color Image Segmentation Using Fuzzy C-Regression Model. Advances in Fuzzy Systems 2017 (2017).
5. Canny, J.: A computational approach to edge detection. IEEE Trans. Pattern Anal Mach Intell 8(6), 679698 (1986)
6. Gonzalez, R.C.,Woods, R.E.: Digital Image Processing. Addison-Wesley, MA (1992)
7. Maini, R., Sohal, J.S.: Performance evaluation of prewitt edge detector for noisy images. ICGST Int. J. Graph.Vis. Image Process. 6(3), 3946 (2006)
8. Marr, D., Hildreth, E.: Theory of edge detection. Proc. R. Soc. Lond. B 207(1167), 187217 (1980)
9. Ari, Samit, Dipak Kumar Ghosh, and Prashant Kumar Mohanty. Edge detection using ACO and F ratio" Signal, Image and Video Processing 8.4 (2014): 625-634.
10. A. Colorni, M. Dorigo and V. Maniezzo, Distributed optimization by ant colonies, Proceedings of ECAL 91, European Conference on Artificial Life, Elsevier Publishing, Amsterdam,1991.

11. Lu, De-Sian, and Chien-Chang Chen. Edge detection improvement by ant colony optimization. Pattern Recognition Letters 29.4 (2008): 416-425.
12. Tian, Jing, Weiyu Yu, and Shengli Xie. An ant colony optimization algorithm for image edge detection. Evolutionary Computation, 2008. CEC 2008.(IEEE World Congress on Computational Intelligence). IEEE Congress on. IEEE, 2008.
13. Min Chen, Simone A. Ludwig and Keqin Li, Clustering in Big Data, Big Data: Management, Architecture, and Processing, (2017) 333-346.
14. Department of Computer Science and Artificial Intelligence at the University of Granada.

Clustering aided Support Vector Machines

Goce Ristanoski[1], Rahul Soni, Sutharshan Rajasegarar[2], James Bailey[3]

[1]Data61, CSIRO, Australia
[2]School of Information Technology, Deakin University, Australia
[3]Department of Computing and Information Systems,
The University of Melbourne, Australia

Abstract: Support Vector Machines (SVMs) have proven to be an effective approach to learning a classifier from complex datasets. However, highly nonhomogeneous data distributions can pose a challenge for SVMs when the underlying dataset comprises clusters of instances with varying mixtures of class labels. To address this challenge we propose a novel approach, called a cluster-supported Support Vector Machine, in which information derived from clustering can be incorporated directly into the SVM learning process. We provide a theoretical derivation to show that when the total empirical loss is expressed in terms of the combined quadratic empirical loss from each cluster, we can still find a formulation of the optimisation problem that is a convex quadratic programming problem. We discuss the scenarios where this type of model would be beneficial, and present empirical evidence that demonstrates the improved accuracy of our combined model.

1. Introduction

Support Vector Machines, built on the concept of margin theory, have become one of the most widely used supervised learning algorithms. SVMs try to maximize the minimum of the geometric margin i.e., the distance between the decision boundary and the instances closest to it. These instances, called support vectors, are typically small in number compared to the total number of instances, and thus a small number of inner products are required to make a prediction on unseen instances. SVMs can be used for both classification and regression, although the work presented in this paper focuses on improving the classification task.

In practice, the distribution of instances from each class can be highly nonhomogeneous. The density of instances can vary throughout the feature space, corresponding to clusters of instances. Moreover, the distribution of labels can vary from one cluster to another, so that one cluster can be rich in instances belonging to one class, while another cluster may contain a majority of instances from a different class. A challenge for SVMs in this context is that while the chosen support vectors may reflect the overall distribution of the dataset, but may not be representative of the distribution in each cluster.

Clustering algorithms have been used as a tool in many data mining tasks, for the purpose of understanding the grouping that exists among the samples in a dataset. Our work focuses on how the combined use of clustering algorithms and SVMs can be used to improve the accuracy of classification on highly nonhomogeneous datasets. Past research has shown that the straightforward approach of dividing the data according to the cluster labelling, and then learning a separate model for each cluster can yield improvements in accuracy. However, our aim is to find a way that these two approaches can be more closely integrated. For this reason, we look for a way to incorporate some of the knowledge from the clustering into the learning process of the SVM.

In particular, we aim to modify the loss function of the SVM to reflect the accuracy within each cluster, so that we minimise the variation in accuracy between clusters. While this provides a way to improve the overall accuracy of classification, the underlying optimisation problem of SVM learning is no longer a quadratic programming problem. However, we provide a theoretical proof that the resulting loss can be upper bounded by a linear combination of simpler expressions, which yields a convex quadratic optimisation problem for training our cluster-supported SVM classifier. In this way, we can use clustering to provide an efficient way of modelling local nonhomogeneity in the underlying data distribution when constructing the SVM.

The contributions of the work presented in this paper are:

- We investigate how SVM models perform in relation to the knowledge provided by clustering algorithms, that is, the clusters that can be assigned to the data.
- We design a way to use the clustering assigned to a given dataset in the learning process of SVM.
- We perform a detailed empirical analysis that gives clear insight of the relation of the type of data and the performance of SVM with incorporated clustering knowledge.

The remainder of the paper is organised as follows: Section 2 describes the Related work in the area of SVM and clustering for classification. We then present the proposed algorithm in Section 3. Section 4 presents the datasets used in the empirical evaluation and the research findings. We conclude into a summary the contributions of the work shown in this paper in Section 5.

2. Related Work

The success of Support Vector Machines (SVMs) in the tasks of classification and regression has led to an increased use of this method over different types of analysis. From time series analysis [1], graph matching [10] and dimensionality reduction [11], SVMs have proven to be more than just a powerful classification tool. Practical application has also motivated research into SVM that speed-up the learning time [2, 4] and are capable of dealing with large data sets [3].

With the emergence of Big Data, processing large data sets has become a greater challenge than before. A version of SVM that screens the data for features that are irrelevant or with very little relevance has been proposed by [8]. A pre-processing stage of looking into samples which are not contributing to the classifier has been suggested by [5]. Related to that, investigating the option of reducing the number of learned support vectors *via* multiple kernels in order to allow for faster testing is a useful approach [12]. Additional optimisation of the mean and variance alongside the empirical loss has been introduced by [31]. Even consideration of the underlying hardware architecture and parallel processing has provided a contribution in the area of SVM optimization [9]. With modifications such as using Dual Coordinate Ascent

[7] and optimising a specific area of the AUC curve [6], the list of benefits SVMs can provide keeps on increasing.

Research into clustering algorithms has witnessed a substantial increase in interest over the recent years as well. With application areas varying from text processing [20], graph clustering [16], time series data [13] [19] and even discrimination aware learning [14], clustering algorithms can provide contributions in the area of classification by itself, and in combination with other learning models. Just like SVMs, clustering algorithms have been modified to cope with high dimensional data in a fast and efficient manner [17]. An important task is also to find clusterings that are easy to interpret [15], in particular when we can have several clusterings over the same dataset [18].

An important research area in which both clustering and SVM methods have been applied is discrimination aware learning. With other methods being investigated [21-23], it is imperative to consider this aspect when testing new methods. Our work not only considers this aspect, but also empirically evaluates the performance of the new method in relation to discrimination aware learning.

SVMs and clustering algorithms have been successfully applied in order to deliver better results. Approaches such as simple clustering of samples and training an SVM model on each cluster [30], to extracting only the most relevant data per cluster [28, 29, 25, 26], have been shown to be beneficial particularly in the case of large datasets [24, 27, 32]. A modification of the SVM learning process itself, rather than the data, is a more challenging process. Our work aims to investigate this direction, and show that the benefits can be significant over a wide range of data types.

3. Cluster Supported SVM

In this section we define the background of standard SVM and formulate the quadratic objective function for our clustering supported SVM.

3.1. Standard SVM

Let $\mathcal{X} \in \mathbb{R}^d$ be the instance space and $\mathcal{Y} = \{+1, -1\}$ the label set. Let $\mathcal{D}$ be an unknown (underlying) distribution over $\mathcal{X} \times \mathcal{Y}$. Assuming an independent and identically (i.i.d) distributed training set of size m:

$$S = \{(\mathbf{x}_1, y_1), (\mathbf{x}_2, y_2), \ldots, (\mathbf{x}_m, y_m)\},$$

the goal of SVM is to learn a function that can be used to predict the labels for future unseen instances.

For SVMs, f is regarded as a linear model, i.e., $f(\mathbf{x}) = \mathbf{w}^T\phi(\mathbf{x})$ where $\mathbf{w}$ is a linear predictor and $\phi(\mathbf{x})$ is a feature mapping of $\mathbf{x}$ induced by a kernel k, i.e., $k(\mathbf{x}_i, \mathbf{x}_j) = \phi(\mathbf{x}_i)^T\phi(\mathbf{x}_j)$. The margin of instance $(\mathbf{x}_i, y_i)$ is formulated as

$$\gamma_i = y_i\mathbf{w}^T\phi(\mathbf{x}_i), \forall i = 1, \ldots, m. \quad (1)$$

It has been shown that in separable cases where the training examples can be separated with the zero error, SVM with hard-margin (or Hard-margin SVM),

$$\min_{\mathbf{w}} \frac{1}{2}\mathbf{w}^T\mathbf{w}$$

$$s.t. y_i \mathbf{w}^T \phi(\mathbf{x}_i) \geq 1, i = 1, \ldots, m,$$

is regarded as the maximization of the minimum margin $\{\min\{\gamma_i\}_{i=1}^{m}\}$.

In non-separable cases where the training examples cannot be separated with the zero error, SVM with soft-margin (or Soft-margin SVM) has been developed,

$$\begin{aligned} \min_{\mathbf{w},\xi} \quad & \frac{1}{2}\mathbf{w}^T\mathbf{w} + C\sum_{i=1}^{m} \xi_i \\ s.t. \quad & y_i \mathbf{w}^T \phi(\mathbf{x}_i) \geq 1 - \xi_i, \\ & \xi_i \geq 0, i = 1, \ldots, m. \end{aligned} \tag{2}$$

where $\boldsymbol{\xi} = [\xi_1, \ldots, \xi_m]^T$ measure the losses of instances, and C is a trade-off parameter. There exists a constant $\bar{C}$ such that (2) can be equivalently reformulated as,

$$\max_{\mathbf{w}} \gamma_0 - \bar{C}\sum_{i=1}^{m} \xi_i$$

$$s.t. \gamma_i \geq \gamma_0 - \xi_i,$$

$$\xi_i \geq 0, i = 1, \ldots, m,$$

where γ_0 is a relaxed minimum margin, and $\bar{C}$ is the trade-off parameter. Note that γ_0 indeed characterizes the top-p minimum margin; hence, SVMs (with both hard-margin and soft-margin) consider only a single-point margin and have not exploited the whole margin distribution.

3.2. Cluster Supported SVM Formulation

Our work originates from the idea of using additional optimisation *via* the introduction of a quadratic mean in the empirical loss, applied on some form of grouping in the data [21]. We formulate a mathematical model that takes the root mean squared value of the quadratic empirical loss per group into account, and use clustering methods as the basis of our grouping strategy. We call this model **CluSVM** which is achieved by modifying the optimization framework proposed by [31]. As the model introduces the margin mean and margin variance, we derive our formulas with these components as well, which can be omitted for a version without their optimization by setting them to zero.

Also since it is known that soft margin SVM outperforms hard margin SVM, we consider the soft margin case in the rest of the derivation to follow. CluSVM is henceforth referred to as soft margin CluSVM.

We define total empirical loss R_{Qemp} in terms of the Root mean square error (RMSE) value of the quadratic empirical loss per group as follows:

$$\begin{aligned} \boldsymbol{R_{Qemp}(\mathbf{w})} &= \sqrt{\frac{1}{k}\sum_{i=1}^{k} f_i^2(\mathbf{w})} \\ \boldsymbol{f_i(\mathbf{w})} &= \frac{1}{n_i}\sum_{j\in n_i} l(\mathbf{w}, \mathbf{x}_j, y_j) \\ \boldsymbol{l(\mathbf{w}, \mathbf{x}_j, y_j)} &= \frac{1}{2}(\mathbf{w}^T\phi(\mathbf{x}_j) - y_j)^2 \\ \sum_{i=1}^{k} n_i &= m \end{aligned} \tag{3}$$

Hence the optimization problem can be written in terms of the RMSE as follows:

$$\begin{aligned} \min_{\mathbf{w},\xi} \quad & \frac{1}{2}\mathbf{w}^T\mathbf{w} + R_{Qemp}(\mathbf{w}) + \lambda_1\hat{\gamma} - \lambda_2\bar{\gamma} + C\textstyle\sum_{i=1}^m \xi_i \\ s.t. \quad & y_i\mathbf{w}^T\phi(\mathbf{x}_i) \geq 1 - \xi_i, \\ & \xi_i \geq 0, i = 1, \dots, m. \end{aligned} \tag{4}$$

where λ_1 and λ_2 are the parameters for trading-off the margin variance $\hat{\gamma}$, margin mean $\bar{\gamma}$ and model complexity. By substituting (3) in (4) we get:

$$\begin{aligned} \min_{\mathbf{w},\xi} \quad & \frac{1}{2}\mathbf{w}^T\mathbf{w} + \sqrt{\frac{1}{k}\textstyle\sum_{i=1}^k \{\frac{1}{n_i}\sum_{j\in n_i} \frac{1}{2}(\mathbf{w}^T\phi(\mathbf{x}_j) - y_j)^2\}^2} \\ & + \frac{2\lambda_1}{m^2}(m\mathbf{w}^T\mathbf{X}\mathbf{X}^T\mathbf{w} - \mathbf{w}^T\mathbf{X}\mathbf{y}\mathbf{y}^T\mathbf{X}^T\mathbf{w}) \\ & - \frac{\lambda_2}{m}(\mathbf{X}\mathbf{y})^T\mathbf{w} + C\textstyle\sum_{i=1}^m \xi_i \\ s.t. \quad & y_i\mathbf{w}^T\phi(\mathbf{x}_i) \geq 1 - \xi_i, \\ & \xi_i \geq 0, i = 1, \dots, m. \end{aligned} \tag{5}$$

The RMSE value of the quadratic empirical loss function per group as defined in (3), (5) turns out to be a fourth order function w.r.t the margin parameter **w**, which is a tedious formulation to fit in Lagrange KKT conditions. To overcome this, we can reformulate it as a quadratic loss w.r.t **w**. The quadratic empirical loss function w.r.t $\{f_i(\mathbf{w}): f_i(\mathbf{w}) \geq 0 \;\; \forall \;\; i = 1,..,k\}$ is upper bounded by its linear combination as follows:

$$\begin{aligned} R_{Qemp}(\mathbf{w}) = \sqrt{\frac{1}{k}\textstyle\sum_{i=1}^k f_i^2(\mathbf{w})} = \\ \sqrt{\textstyle\sum_{i=1}^k (\frac{f_i(\mathbf{w})}{\sqrt{k}})^2} \approx \textstyle\sum_{i=1}^k \frac{f_i(\mathbf{w})}{\sqrt{k}} \end{aligned} \tag{6}$$

Since $R_{Qemp}(\mathbf{w})$ is upper bounded by the R.H.S of (6), a minimizer of the R.H.S of (6) with respect to parameters $a_i \geq 0, i = 1,..,k$ also leads to the minimization of $R_{emp}(\mathbf{w})$. This means that $R_{Qemp}(\mathbf{w})$ is modelled in terms of the margin parameter $\boldsymbol{\alpha}$ as follows:

$$\begin{aligned} R_{Qemp}(\mathbf{w}) &= \sqrt{\frac{1}{k}\textstyle\sum_{i=1}^k f_i^2(\mathbf{w})} \\ &= \sqrt{\textstyle\sum_{i=1}^k (\frac{f_i(\mathbf{w})}{\sqrt{k}})^2} \approx \textstyle\sum_{i=1}^k \frac{f_i(\mathbf{w})}{\sqrt{k}} \\ R_{Qemp}(\mathbf{w}) &\approx \textstyle\sum_{i=1}^k \frac{1}{n_i\sqrt{k}}\sum_{j\in n_i} l(\mathbf{w},\mathbf{x}_j,y_j) \end{aligned} \tag{7}$$

The optimal solution form of **w** leads to the following representation of quadratic loss $l(\mathbf{w},\mathbf{x}_j,y_j)$ in terms of the inner product of the kernel matrix **G** and solution vector $\boldsymbol{\alpha}$:

$$
\begin{aligned}
l(\mathbf{w}, \mathbf{x}_j, y_j) &= \frac{1}{2}(\mathbf{w}^T\phi(\mathbf{x}_j) - y_j)^2 \\
&= \frac{1}{2}\{\mathbf{w}^T\phi(\mathbf{x}_j)\}^2 - \mathbf{w}^T\phi(\mathbf{x}_j)y_j + \frac{1}{2} \\
&= \frac{1}{2}\mathbf{w}^T\phi(\mathbf{x}_j)\phi(\mathbf{x}_j)^T\mathbf{w} - \mathbf{w}^T\phi(\mathbf{x}_j)y_j + \frac{1}{2} \\
&= \frac{1}{2}\alpha^T\mathbf{X}^T\phi(\mathbf{x}_j)\phi(\mathbf{x}_j)^T\mathbf{X}\alpha - \\
&\quad \alpha^T\mathbf{X}^T\phi(\mathbf{x}_j)y_j + \frac{1}{2} \\
&= \frac{1}{2}\alpha^T\mathbf{G}_{:j}\mathbf{G}_{:j}^T\alpha - \alpha^T\mathbf{G}_{:j}y_j + \frac{1}{2}
\end{aligned}
\tag{8}
$$

where $\mathbf{G}_{:i}$ denotes the i-th column of $\mathbf{G}$ as before.

4. Experiments and Results

Evaluation of the performance of the newly proposed CluSVM focuses on determining what features of the dataset and the clustering contribute to the actual change in performance. For that purpose we generated a series of datasets in which we introduced a range for some of the features that would describe the performance of the model in relation to the nature of the data. This generation of datasets allows for more indepth analysis of how the clusters structure, proximity and densitiy are relevant to the final model performance.

4.1. Dataset Description

We generated a total of 54 synthetic datasets, each with 7 numeric attributes in the range of 0-600, and 5000 samples per dataset. For half of the datasets, we generated clusters in such a way that 2 clusters would not overlap in any of the 7 features. This was accomplished by setting the cluster boundary at half of the minimal allowed distance between two cluster centres, and generating all the data for a given cluster within the cluster boundary. The other 27 datasets were generated in a similar manner, except that for each feature per cluster, the cluster boundary for that feature was set to 2/3 of the allowed minimal distance between cluster centres. This means that in some of the feature spaces, it is possible to have an overlap between 2 clusters, but that overlap will not be a region with the greatest number of samples for each of the clusters overlapping. Furthermore, 75% of the samples were randomly assigned around the cluster centre within the cluster boundary, and the remaining 25% of the samples were assigned closer to the cluster centres at a maximum distance of one half of the cluster boundary, for more concentrated cluster centre areas.
The clusters and cluster labels in the datasets were generated in the range of the following attributes:

- Positive sample rate - the ratio of positive vs negative samples in real life datasets is rarely 1:1. Quite often we are concerned with situations where the class of interest is the less present class in the dataset. As mentioned in the related work section of the paper, research in determining the effect of unbalanced datasets is of significance in the data mining area. For that purpose, we generate datasets where the rate of positive samples in the dataset is 0.5, 0.4 and 0.25 (a rate of 0.5 means that 50% of the samples are from the class).

- Number of clusters - we aim to investigate how the number of clusters contributes to the prediction accuracy. Our initial assumption was that with fewer clusters, the difference in performance between our method and the standard method would not be as significant as when the number of clusters was higher. We also aimed to investigate whether a large number of samples in the dataset results in lower accuracy on its own. For that purpose, we generated datasets with 5, 10 and 15 clusters within the same feature space.
- Cluster homogeneity - the cluster label will correspond to the most frequently occurring class of samples in that cluster. Clusters that only have samples from one class would be ideal, but this is far from expected. By varying the presence of the most frequent class, we can investigate if considering the grouping strategy will still provide a contribution when the cluster homogeneity is lower. The cluster homogeneity was set to 0.7, 0.8 and 0.9 (0.9 corresponds to 90% of the samples in that cluster belonging to the same class, which is the class assigned to the cluster itself).

By varying each of these three attributes, each with three different values, we end up with 27 different combinations corresponding to each of the two groups of 27 datasets generated.
The metrics used to evaluate the performance of the new algorithm are Accuracy (number of correctly classified samples/number of samples), as well as Recall and F-score for the positive samples: Recall=True Positive/(True Positive+False Negative), F-score=2*Precision*Recall/(Precision+Recall), Precision=True Positive/(True Positive+ False Positive). The Recall and F-score indicate how many of the samples with positive class labels have been classified correctly, which is significant in particular for the changes we investigate in the positive sample rate.
The Wilcoxon signed rank test (WSRT p-value) is used for the Accuracy, Recall and F-score values between our method and each of the other baseline methods are used to determine whether the changes are significant enough. We compared our method CluSVM with naive Bayes (NB), Polynomial Kernel SVM (SVM), Normalized Polynomial Kernel SVM (SVM NPK), and Multilayer Perceptron ANN (MLP).

4.2. Datasets with Overlapping Cluster Boundary

Presented in Table **2** are the results on the 27 datasets where no clear boundary between the clusters were set, and it was possible for some samples to overlap with others in some of the features. This is why when testing our CluSVM model, we used a KNN algorithm to set the cluster labels and include the clusters overlap information, rather then using our original clustering labels. In a few of the cases, this resulted in 2 close clusters with the same label being labelled as 1 cluster, resulting in a total of 14 clusters, which was still considered to fall in the 15 clusters category.
We can see that in most of the cases, particularly when having 10 and 15 clusters, our methods shows the best results from all metrics: Accuracy, Recall and F-score. MLP

is a close runner up, while NB, SVM and even SVM NPK are all outperformed by CluSVM. An interesting observation is that the number of clusters is quite relevant to the performance of all the models: with 5 clusters per dataset the difference in performance between the models is not as great as when we have 10 and 15 clusters. This can be especially seen in the decrease of the Recall and F-score values for most of the baseline comparison methods as we increase the number of clusters.

The cluster homogeneity behaviour seems to be consistent for all three cases of 5, 10 and 15 clusters: the lower the cluster homogeneity, the lower the performance for all methods. The positive sample rate seems to have a greater impact in the cases when we have a small number of clusters, and seems less relevant when the number of clusters is higher. Figure **1** shows the accuracy per cluster for the case of cluster homogeneity=0.7, positive sample rate=0.4, 15 clusters. The variance in per cluster accuracy is handled by our CluSVM method, and we can see there is a large difference in the per cluster accuracy for most of the remaining methods.

4.3. Datasets with clear cluster boundary

Table **1** shows the results of testing the 27 datasets with clear cluster boundaries, in which case we used the original cluster labels in our CluSVM. In this case, the positive sample rate seems to be more relevant, as the sample rate of 0.25 shows that MLP is slightly better than our CluSVM in Accuracy, and has more cases of higher values for Recall and F-Score. Still, our CluSVM seems to be the preferred method when compared in general to all the baseline methods.

The same conclusion that the number of clusters plays a significant role can be derived in this scenario as well - the differences of the Recall and F-score in datasets with 10 and 15 clusters is a clear indicator of the advantages our clustering aided method can deliver.

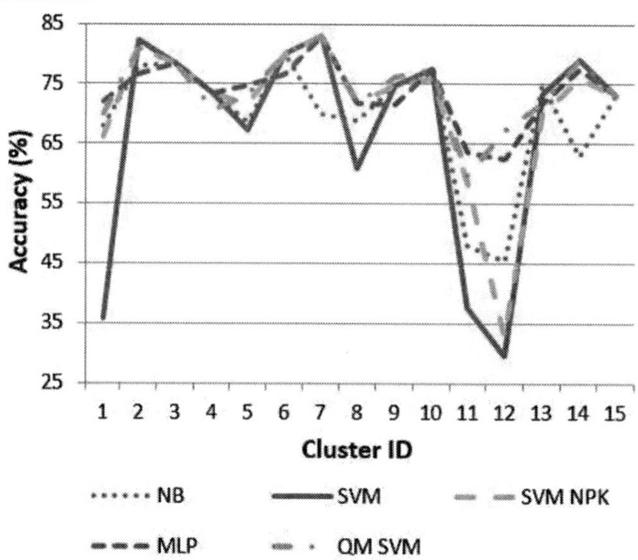

Figure 1. Individual cluster accuracy for all methods.

5. Conclusion

This paper investigates the performance of some of SVM learning methods when clustering is applied on the samples, and suggests a strategy of how to incorporate clustering information directly in the learning process. The CluSVM model with quadratic mean empirical loss has the flexibility to use any type of grouping, and suits the purpose of investigating the performance of this clustering supported model quite well. We have observed an increase in several performance metrics which demonstrates the combination of the two learning models is possible in a more complex, yet still straightforward way.

Table 1. Performance metrics for datasets with overlapping of cluster boundaries. Our proposed CluSVM shows to have statistically significant improvements compared to NB, SVM and SVM NPK, and still better performance when compared to MLP.

		Accuracy (%)					Recall					F-score				
Num. clus.	Cluster hmg.	NB	SVM	SVM NPK	MLP	Clu-SVM	NB	SVM	SVM NPK	MLP	Clu-SVM	NB	SVM	SVM NPK	MLP	Clu-SVM
Positive sample rate = 0.5																
5	0.7	60.5	58.3	62.4	63.1	62.5	0.639	0.598	0.572	0.57	0.564	0.615	0.586	0.6	0.604	0.597
	0.8	66.4	64.1	70.8	67.5	70.6	0.653	0.615	0.627	0.701	0.633	0.659	0.63	0.681	0.682	0.682
	0.9	69.7	69.3	78.2	76.3	77.7	0.694	0.682	0.698	0.725	0.692	0.689	0.683	0.756	0.748	0.75
10	0.7	63.3	58.9	67.6	64.1	68.8	0.633	0.72	0.68	0.776	0.702	0.639	0.632	0.623	0.679	0.688
	0.8	71.6	68.8	78.3	77.8	78.7	0.694	0.771	0.775	0.783	0.783	0.707	0.709	0.779	0.777	0.784
	0.9	79.1	76.2	88.5	89.4	89.8	0.741	0.759	0.883	0.887	0.889	0.782	0.763	0.886	0.894	0.898
15	0.7	66.9	66.1	69	69.4	70.1	0.611	0.605	0.661	0.713	0.724	0.64	0.632	0.672	0.692	0.699
	0.8	74.9	74.9	78.8	80.1	80.3	0.698	0.714	0.792	0.832	0.834	0.736	0.74	0.788	0.807	0.809
	0.9	83.4	85.1	91	91.7	92.2	0.765	0.815	0.925	0.935	0.944	0.827	0.851	0.914	0.921	0.926
Positive sample rate = 0.4																
5	0.7	73	69.4	72.8	73.1	74	0.602	0.477	0.546	0.615	0.638	0.636	0.55	0.611	0.615	0.658
	0.8	80.4	74.2	80.7	81.1	81.6	0.729	0.61	0.694	0.783	0.751	0.733	0.636	0.725	0.754	0.751
	0.9	84.2	78.1	86.3	86.5	88.28	0.772	0.67	0.779	0.855	0.824	0.794	0.707	0.818	0.824	0.847
10	0.7	68.3	70	74.9	74.5	75.5	0.479	0.485	0.668	0.688	0.687	0.541	0.558	0.68	0.677	0.684
	0.8	72.7	75.5	84.2	84.1	84.6	0.609	0.584	0.815	0.815	0.818	0.635	0.649	0.8	0.799	0.805
	0.9	77.1	78.4	91.2	91.7	91.6	0.669	0.642	0.891	0.894	0.894	0.703	0.707	0.891	0.897	0.896
15	0.7	69.4	67.4	71.2	73.6	74.1	0.535	0.328	0.522	0.603	0.643	0.587	0.45	0.596	0.65	0.668
	0.8	74	71.2	78.6	81.7	82.4	0.639	0.455	0.621	0.748	0.753	0.665	0.561	0.701	0.768	0.776
	0.9	78.4	75.6	85.4	90.5	90.9	0.722	0.526	0.727	0.864	0.869	0.729	0.635	0.801	0.88	0.885
Positive sample rate = 0.25																
5	0.7	82.5	82.2	80.5	82.2	82	0.569	0.554	0.446	0.58	0.5	0.636	0.626	0.552	0.637	0.6
	0.8	86.4	86.1	85.2	86.3	85.6	0.644	0.633	0.607	0.64	0.593	0.722	0.715	0.693	0.72	0.694
	0.9	91	91.1	89.7	91	89.5	0.716	0.709	0.705	0.709	0.673	0.802	0.802	0.777	0.8	0.765
10	0.7	79.4	75.3	81.3	81.6	81.7	0.332	NA	0.445	0.506	0.51	0.443	NA	0.541	0.576	0.579
	0.8	83.7	84.1	85.7	85.7	86.1	0.464	0.506	0.59	0.59	0.602	0.577	0.603	0.664	0.664	0.674
	0.9	85.1	86.5	89.4	89.7	89.6	0.517	0.61	0.688	0.68	0.684	0.651	0.708	0.777	0.78	0.78
15	0.7	78.3	74.1	80.8	86	86.4	0.259	NA	0.409	0.683	0.707	0.382	NA	0.525	0.717	0.729
	0.8	81.9	80.3	88	90.4	91.3	0.39	0.321	0.623	0.795	0.811	0.527	0.457	0.738	0.811	0.828
	0.9	86.3	85.5	94.2	95.8	95.2	0.498	0.478	0.865	0.948	0.94	0.646	0.623	0.882	0.919	0.908
WSRT p-value		<0.0001			0.008	base	<0.001			0.5	base	<0.0001			0.11	base

Future research directions in this are can include other types of grouping strategies, including the adaptation of some form of grouping for datasets that have proven to be more difficult to learn, such as datasets with possible noise, outliers and distribution based grouping.

Table 2. Performance metrics for datasets without overlapping of cluster boundaries. We can observe similar results as with the case of overlapping boundaries, with our CluSVM showing to outperform other methods in most cases.

		Accuracy (%)					Recall					F-score				
Num. clus.	Cluster hmg.	NB	SVM	SVM NPK	MLP	Clu-SVM	NB	SVM	SVM NPK	MLP	Clu-SVM	NB	SVM	SVM NPK	MLP	Clu-SVM
Positive sample rate = 0.5																
5	0.7	63.1	62.3	64.7	63.2	**65.3**	0.605	0.583	0.564	**0.609**	0.593	0.626	0.613	0.62	0.628	**0.634**
	0.8	71.2	71.4	**73.4**	74.2	**73.4**	0.687	0.687	0.667	**0.689**	0.671	0.709	0.711	0.719	**0.732**	0.721
	0.9	78	75.8	80.7	**81.7**	80.7	0.742	0.706	0.725	**0.739**	0.731	0.78	0.754	0.798	**0.809**	0.799
10	0.7	63.5	61.8	67.5	67	**68.1**	0.625	0.592	0.625	**0.667**	0.665	0.628	0.605	0.655	0.666	**0.673**
	0.8	71.8	70.5	76.6	77	**78.1**	0.724	0.699	0.742	0.754	**0.76**	0.716	0.7	0.757	0.763	**0.774**
	0.9	80.2	77.8	**86.6**	88.5	**88.6**	0.835	0.807	0.879	**0.895**	0.887	0.809	0.785	0.868	**0.887**	**0.887**
15	0.7	63.1	59.3	68.1	68.9	**70.1**	0.736	0.726	0.732	0.716	**0.734**	0.665	0.64	0.695	0.696	**0.701**
	0.8	68.7	61.5	79	80.4	**81.6**	0.796	0.738	**0.835**	0.826	**0.835**	0.711	0.65	0.794	0.803	**0.815**
	0.9	76.8	69.4	88.7	90.9	**92.1**	0.862	0.807	0.912	0.921	**0.941**	0.785	0.721	0.888	0.909	**0.921**
Positive sample rate = 0.4																
5	0.7	72.2	69.1	73.7	74	**76.3**	0.575	0.455	0.996	**0.683**	0.681	0.622	0.54	0.643	0.677	**0.696**
	0.8	79	76.2	82	**83**	82.8	0.695	0.622	0.751	**0.776**	0.766	0.724	0.675	0.768	**0.784**	0.78
	0.9	84	80.1	90.7	90.4	**91.4**	0.747	0.683	0.874	0.878	**0.885**	0.796	0.742	0.887	0.885	**0.896**
10	0.7	69.3	66.2	71.3	75.6	**76.2**	0.525	0.369	0.515	0.676	**0.696**	0.58	0.469	0.592	0.691	**0.703**
	0.8	77.5	69.3	82.6	84.4	**84.5**	0.658	0.454	0.742	0.812	**0.817**	0.691	0.531	0.766	0.799	**0.802**
	0.9	82.3	72.9	89.4	90.9	**91.1**	0.711	0.773	0.835	0.859	**0.86**	0.748	0.679	0.854	0.875	**0.877**
15	0.7	65.7	69.9	70.7	74	**75**	0.462	0.503	0.485	0.674	**0.687**	0.516	0.569	0.567	0.672	**0.685**
	0.8	70.3	76	79.8	81.9	**83.9**	0.542	0.59	0.657	0.761	**0.791**	0.595	0.664	0.723	0.772	**0.798**
	0.9	75.5	80.9	87.8	90.4	**91.4**	0.639	0.682	0.804	0.868	**0.886**	0.677	0.742	0.841	0.879	**0.892**
Positive sample rate = 0.25																
5	0.7	**82.5**	82.8	81.8	81.7	81.9	0.512	0.496	0.46	**0.524**	0.478	**0.592**	0.589	0.556	0.587	0.572
	0.8	85	84.7	84.9	**85.8**	85.4	0.572	0.544	0.552	**0.589**	0.573	0.648	0.631	0.638	**0.667**	0.654
	0.9	89.5	89.3	89.9	89.8	**90.2**	**0.695**	0.659	0.687	0.687	0.683	0.767	0.754	0.772	0.77	**0.776**
10	0.7	79	73.9	78.2	81.5	**81.8**	0.314	0	0.237	**0.448**	0.444	0.439	NA	0.363	**0.589**	0.561
	0.8	82	72.2	82.2	**85.3**	84.9	0.493	0	0.478	**0.604**	0.579	0.604	NA	0.599	**0.696**	0.681
	0.9	86.4	84.8	87.4	**89.6**	88.6	0.579	0.518	0.615	**0.676**	0.66	0.677	0.628	0.707	**0.763**	0.741
15	0.7	80.2	75.1	83	**85.6**	84.3	0.337	0	0.518	**0.703**	0.615	0.459	NA	0.603	**0.708**	0.661
	0.8	84	83.8	88	89.1	**89.2**	0.483	0.504	0.701	0.735	**0.744**	0.586	0.593	0.732	0.759	**0.763**
	0.9	86.4	84	93.4	**95.4**	95.1	0.61	0.583	0.89	**0.941**	0.917	0.695	0.649	0.873	**0.912**	0.905
WSRT p-value		<0.0001			0.0366	base	<0.0001			0.588	base	<0.0001			0.84	base

REFERENCES

[1] Muller, K. R., Smola, A. J., Ratsch, G., Scholkopf, B., Kohlmorgen, J. and Vapnik, V. (1999). Using support vector machines for time series prediction. Advances in kernel methodsâ€"support vector learning, MIT Press, Cambridge, MA, 243-254.

[2] SchÃ¶lkopf, B., Simard, P., Vapnik, V. and Smola, A.J., 1997. Improving the accuracy and speed of support vector machines. Advances in neural information processing systems, 9, pp.375-381.

[3] Fan, R. E., Chang, K. W., Hsieh, C. J., Wang, X. R. and Lin, C. J. (2008). LIBLINEAR: A library for large linear classification. Journal of machine learning research, 9(Aug), 1871-1874.

[4] Hsieh, C. J., Chang, K. W., Lin, C. J., Keerthi, S. S. and Sundararajan, S. (2008, July). A dual coordinate descent method for large-scale linear SVM. In Proceedings of the 25th international conference on Machine learning (pp. 408-415). ACM.

[5] Ogawa, K., Suzuki, Y. and Takeuchi, I. (2013). Safe Screening of Non-Support Vectors in Pathwise SVM Computation. In ICML (3) (pp. 1382-1390).

[6] Narasimhan, H. and Agarwal, S. (2013, June). A Structural SVM Based Approach for Optimizing Partial AUC. In ICML (1) (pp. 516-524).

[7] Shalev-Shwartz, S. and Zhang, T. (2013). Stochastic dual coordinate ascent methods for regularized loss minimization. Journal of Machine Learning Research, 14(Feb), 567-599.

[8] Zhao, Z., Liu, J. and Cox, J. (2014, August). Safe and efficient screening for sparse support vector machine. In Proceedings of the 20th ACM SIGKDD international conference on Knowledge discovery and data mining (pp. 542-551). ACM.

[9] Matsushima, S., Vishwanathan, S. V. N. and Smola, A. J. (2012, August). Linear support vector machines *via* dual cached loops. In Proceedings of the 18th ACM SIGKDD international conference on Knowledge discovery and data mining (pp. 177-185). ACM.

[10] Caetano, T. S., McAuley, J. J., Cheng, L., Le, Q. V. and Smola, A. J. (2009). Learning graph matching. IEEE transactions on pattern analysis and machine intelligence, 31(6), 1048-1058.

[11] Tao, Q., Chu, D. and Wang, J. (2008). Recursive support vector machines for dimensionality reduction. IEEE Transactions on Neural Networks, 19(1), 189-193.

[12] Hu, M., Chen, Y. and Kwok, J. T. Y. (2009). Building sparse multiple-kernel SVM classifiers. IEEE Transactions on Neural Networks, 20(5), 827-839.

[13] Meesrikamolkul, W., Niennattrakul, V. and Ratanamahatana, C. A. (2012, May). Shape-based clustering for time series data. In Pacific-Asia Conference on Knowledge Discovery and Data Mining (pp. 530-541). Springer Berlin Heidelberg.

[14] Luong, B. T., Ruggieri, S. and Turini, F. (2011, August). k-NN as an implementation of situation testing for discrimination discovery and prevention. In Proceedings of the 17th ACM SIGKDD international conference on Knowledge discovery and data mining (pp. 502-510). ACM.

[15] Chan, J., Leckie, C., Bailey, J. and Ramamohanarao, K. (2014, December). TRIBAC: Discovering interpretable clusters and latent structures in graphs. In 2014 IEEE International Conference on Data Mining (pp. 737-742). IEEE.

[16] Yang, W., SG, E. and Xu, H. (2015). A Divide and Conquer Framework for Distributed Graph Clustering. In Proceedings of the 32nd International Conference on Machine Learning (ICML-15) (pp. 504-513).

[17] Yi, J., Zhang, L., Wang, J., Jin, R. and Jain, A. K. (2014). A Single-Pass Algorithm for Efficiently Recovering Sparse Cluster Centers of High-dimensional Data. In ICML (pp. 658-666).

[18] Romano, S., Bailey, J., Nguyen, X. V. and Verspoor, K. (2014, June). Standardized Mutual Information for Clustering Comparisons: One Step Further in Adjustment for Chance. In ICML (pp. 1143-1151).

[19] Dzeroski, S., Gjorgjioski, V., Slavkov, I. and Struyf, J. (2006, September). Analysis of time series data with predictive clustering trees. In International Workshop on Knowledge Discovery in Inductive Databases (pp. 63-80). Springer Berlin Heidelberg.

[20] Yin, J. and Wang, J. (2014, August). A dirichlet multinomial mixture model-based approach for short text clustering. In Proceedings of the 20th ACM SIGKDD international conference on Knowledge discovery and data mining (pp. 233-242). ACM.

[21] Liu, W. and Chawla, S. (2011, January). A Quadratic Mean based Supervised Learning Model for Managing Data Skewness. In SDM (pp. 188-198).

[22] Calders, T. and Verwer, S. (2010). Three naive Bayes approaches for discrimination-free classification. Data Mining and Knowledge Discovery, 21(2), 277-292.

[23] Kamishima, T., Akaho, S., Asoh, H. and Sakuma, J. (2012, September). Fairness-aware classifier with prejudice remover regularizer. In Joint European Conference on Machine Learning and Knowledge Discovery in Databases (pp. 35-50). Springer Berlin Heidelberg.

[24] Yu, H., Yang, J. and Han, J. (2003, August). Classifying large data sets using SVMs with hierarchical clusters. In Proceedings of the ninth ACM SIGKDD international conference on Knowledge discovery and data mining (pp. 306-315). ACM.

[25] Li, D. C. and Fang, Y. H. (2008). An algorithm to cluster data for efficient classification of support vector machines. Expert Systems with Applications, 34(3), 2013-2018.

[26] De Almeida, M. B., de PÃ¡dua Braga, A. and Braga, J. P. (2000). SVM-KM: speeding SVMs learning with a priori cluster selection and k-means. In Neural Networks, 2000. Proceedings. Sixth Brazilian Symposium on (pp. 162-167). IEEE.

[27] Shin, H. and Cho, S. (2007). Neighborhood propertyâ€"based pattern selection for support vector machines. Neural Computation, 19(3), 816-855.

[28] Wang, W. and Xu, Z. (2004). A heuristic training for support vector regression. Neurocomputing, 61, 259-275.

[29] Guo, G. and Zhang, J. S. (2007). Reducing examples to accelerate support vector regression. Pattern Recognition Letters, 28(16), 2173-2183.

[30] GarcÃ-a-Pedrajas, N. (2009). Constructing ensembles of classifiers by means of weighted instance selection. IEEE Transactions on Neural Networks, 20(2), 258-277.

[31] Zhang, T. and Zhou, Z. H. (2014, August). Large margin distribution machine. In Proceedings of the 20th ACM SIGKDD international conference on Knowledge discovery and data mining (pp. 313-322). ACM.

[32] Gu, Quanquan and Jiawei Han. Clustered Support Vector Machines. In AISTATS, pp. 307-315. 2013

Implementation of Machine Learning Techniques for Crime Classification and Prediction

Richa Pandey, Rajeshwari Sah, Poornima Kulkarni

R.V. College of Engineering, Bangalore, India
richa6677@gmail.com, rajeshwari.sah@gmail.com, poornimapk@rvce.edu.in

Abstract. There has been an enormous increase in crime rate in the recent past. Any significant research to predict, prevent or solve the crime is a progressive step in making the society safer and peaceful. Understanding the crime and its patterns efficiently and accurately is becoming challenging with respect to the increasing volumes of crime related data. Techniques like machine learning help in a better analysis of the crime patterns and can be used to classify and predict the crime on the basis of such analysis. This paper presents an intelligent crime classification and prediction system using various machine learning techniques. The system compares and tests these learning techniques which is further supported by results that show the effectiveness of the system and suggests future advancements in the same. The best accuracy achieved among all the algorithms is 93% for a 39-way classification using Support Vector Machines.

Keywords: Crime data analysis, Machine Learning, Classification, Prediction.

1. Introduction

With the growing crime rates, analysis of patterns and prediction of crime has become a necessity in today's world. It has a vast scope and can provide assistance to both police and general public. The government to keep track of and have a better understanding of crime in the state can use it. Public safety and concerns can be ensured at a higher level. Civilians can be made aware of the most probable crime that can take place in their area at a particular time, further, they can take precautionary measures for themselves. The government can use this knowledge to run targeted and sensitive practices to mitigate crime in their state.

Machine learning involves learning from previous data by training it through one or more algorithms and concentrating on prediction which is established on experienced properties after training. We have designed an intelligent system that trains itself on a huge set of crime data and eventually predicts the crime based on any given instance of time frame and location.

In this paper, we aim at exploiting various machine learning techniques such as naïve Bayes, decision tree, random forest and support vector machines (SVM) to classify and predict the type of crimes [1], for San Francisco region. All of these methods yield different accuracies, the highest belonging to SVM. The accuracy of SVM was enhanced when we moved from Gaussian kernel to a linear kernel.

The training data is collected from Kaggle [7] and it contains 39 different categories of crimes. After its preprocessing, the classifier is trained on the data. Once the training is completed, for a given user input (contains time frame and location) probabilities are calculated for all 39 crime categories. The category containing the highest probability is the predicted crime for the given instance. Log loss value, accuracy and confusion matrix are considered as evaluation metrics of the system [3]. Visualisations involving graphs help in a better analysis of the accuracies of the algorithms and calculated probabilities of all the different categories of crime whereas interactive maps putting crime patterns and hot spots on display. The approach followed in preprocessing of data and all the various algorithms have been briefly discussed further.

2. Problem Statement

Our goal is to predict the type of crime in a given area at any given time frame with reasonable accuracy. After formulating the problem, we define and discuss the features that we have got from our data source, then preprocessing it to obtain all required crime data, which clearly shows the relevant features.
Crime classification involves the use of learning of classifiers over collected training data. After training, we aim to predict the category of crime that is most likely to occur at the given instance. The comparison and enhancement of accuracies of the classifiers is a major concern.

3. Methodology

The different modules incorporated within the system are Data preprocessor, Classifier, Predictor and Data visualizer.
The data that is used, belongs to San Francisco criminal record available through Kaggle datasets [7], spans over 12 years (2003-2015). There are separate sets of training and testing data. The training data set contains crime information which is segregated and organised as date, time, day of the week, category of crime (that occurred at the corresponding date and time), small description of the crime, corresponding police district, location of crime (complete address, corresponding latitude and longitude). The testing data set contains all of the above information except the crime category. There are up to 900000 records in a CSV (comma separated values) format.
The crime has been classified up to 39 different categories, some of which are arson, assault, burglary, extortion, forgery, kidnapping, larceny, robbery, trespass, gambling, vandalism etc.

3.1. Preprocessing

There is a need to trim, scale and normalise the input data. The training data file is read by a CSV reader library into a table. This data is then encoded into a DataFrame object. Textual data such as day of week, district etc. are encoded into a numeric representation. The feature extractor takes the relevant features such as the location of the crime, in terms of latitude and longitude, the date and time of the incident, and the day of the week. Since the data set is huge and does not correspond to an origin, this data is normalised to the mean values. Since all the data set collected should be fed to the classifier in an efficient way, the two-dimensional array is transformed into a sparse matrix. Sparse matrices are used for better storage and to avoid the potential memory access irregularities. Compressed Sparse Row (CSR) has been used as the matrix storage format. Apart from decreasing the needed storage/memory space, CSR also increases the computational speed as only non-empty elements as only non-empty elements are involved in the matrix operations.

3.2. Machine Learning Techniques

Machine learning involves the design of algorithms that can learn from data and hence make predictions on it. Such algorithms make data-driven predictions by building a model from sample inputs.

We have used the corresponding implementations of the learning techniques that are publicly through the Scikit-learn machine learning framework in Python [8]. The techniques that are mentioned below were applied to the normalised data that we had obtained after preprocessing.

Naïve Bayes. This is an easy and fast technique based on Bayes' Theorem, with an assumption of independence among features. This assumption rightly matches with our crime data sets.

We have used Gaussian naïve Bayes, as we are dealing with continuous data which are distributed according to the Gaussian distribution [2].

$$y = \underset{k \in \{1,2,3,\ldots,39\}}{argmax}\; p(C_k)\prod_{i=1}^{4} p(x_i \mid C_k) \quad (1)$$

where,

$C_1, C_2,..,C_{39}$ represents the 39 categories of crime x_1,x_2,x_3,x_4 represents feature set, considering crime timestamp, day of week, police district and location (latitude and longitude)

The Bayes classifier constructed from the probability model assigns class label y $= C_k$ for some k, (considering that each feature F_i is conditionally independent of every other feature F_j for $j \neq$, given any category C) is shown in the equation 1.

Decision Tree. Decision tree learning involves the formation of a decision tree from class-labelled training tuples. assuming that all of the features have finite discrete domains, and there is a single target feature called the classification. Each element of the domain of the classification is called a class.

A decision tree is a tree in which each internal node is labelled with an input feature. The arcs coming from a node labelled with a feature are labeled with each of the possible values of the feature. Each leaf of the tree is labelled with a probability distribution over the classes. Classification tree analysis is followed by our crime data.

Random Forest. It operates by constructing many decision trees at training time and outputting the class that is the mode of the classes (classification) or mean prediction (regression) of the individual trees.

Random decision forests correct for decision trees' nature of overfitting to their training set. It also combines random selection of training data sets. This bootstrapping procedure leads to better performance because it decreases the variance of the model, without increasing the bias.

Support Vector Machines. An SVM model involves the representation of data sets mapped as points in space, so that the data of separate categories are divided by a clear gap, which should be as wide as possible. The test data are then mapped into the same space and then predicted to belong to a category based on which side of the gap they were mapped.

Firstly, we incorporated Gaussian (RBF-Radial Basis Function) kernel which uses normal curves around data points [6]. After this we used an alternate option, replacing RBF with Linear Kernel, and found better accuracies. Linear kernel is faster and performs better with our data sets.

The basic representation of Linear Kernel is shown in the equation 2 below, where X and y are data sets:

$$K(X, Y) = X^{T}Y. \tag{2}$$

3.3. System Input and Output

Input. 1 or more inputs including time frames and location for which prediction is to be made (or a Test data set), Training data set.
Output. Accuracy graphs of all learning methods (using Matplotlib), Crime pattern visualisation and comparison against different parameters, two interactive San Francisco map (using google map API), one that displays crime hot spots based on training data set and the other that takes a user input and visualises the predicted crimes.

3.4. Evaluation Metrics

The criteria for testing different algorithms are log loss, confusion matrix and accuracy score. Log loss, ranging between 0 and 1, shows the uncertainty of the probabilities of different models by comparing them to their corresponding true labels. Similarly, a confusion matrix is the matrix representation of the predicted and the actual class. Accuracy score, calculated after the confusion matrix is displayed, determines the ratio of number of correctly predicted values to the total number of predicted values.

3.5. User Interface Paradigm

The GUI designed using Tkinter [9] comprises of options like selecting the classifier to run, choosing the training data file, viewing the graphs and exploring the map. It comprises of a menu selection system, which the user can select.
The textual output displaying the evaluation metrics of all the crime categories are shown in the Python shell along with separate visualisations windows of corresponding graphs and maps.

4. Result and Evaluation

The results obtained have been briefly discussed in this section.

4.1. Evaluation metrics

The sample evaluation metrics of all the learning techniques have been shown in Table **1**. Each metrics shows the log loss value, accuracy and confusion matrix generated during the learning of a technique corresponding to a chosen category of crime.

Table 1. Sample evaluation metrics corresponding to Decision Tree, Naïve Bayes, Random Forest and SVM

Decision Tree Learning: LARCENY/THEFT log loss: 7.25322060388 accuracy: 0.79 Confusion matrix : [[702 97] [113 88]]	Naive Bayes Learning: ARSON log loss: 5.55087477775 accuracy: 0.839285714286 Confusion matrix : [[423 0] [81 0]]
Random Forest Learning: FORGERY/COUNTERFEITING log loss: 3.90288173262 accuracy: 0.887 Confusion matrix : [[799 0] [113 88]]	SVM (RBF kernel) Learning: MISSING PERSON log loss: 3.3848000867 accuracy: 0.902 Confusion matrix : [[803 0] [98 99]]
SVM (Linear kernel) Learning: BURGLARY log loss: 1.208862771 accuracy: 0.965 Confusion matrix : [[804 7] [28 161]]	

4.2. Accuracy Graphs

The accuracies of all the techniques have been visualized through separate graphs which are shown from Fig. **1** to Fig. 5. It can be observed that the accuracy seems to increase as me move from decision tree to naïve Bayes. Further increase is observed from random forest to SVM. Linear kernel SVM shows more accuracy than RBF kernel SVM.

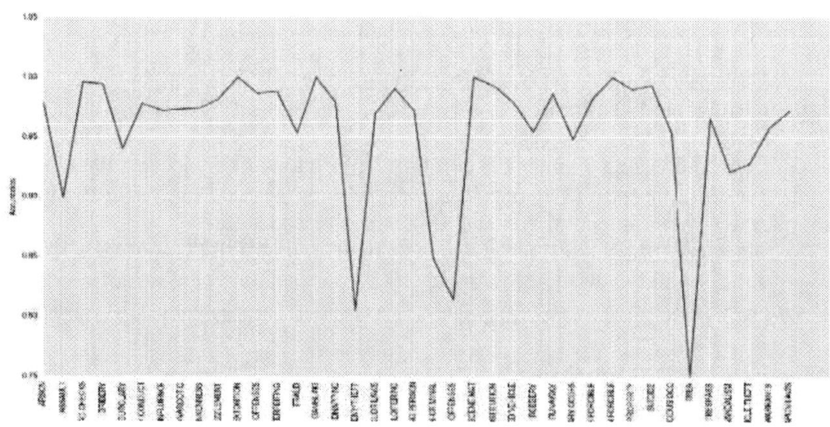

Fig. 1. Accuracy graph of decision tree for all 39 categories of crime

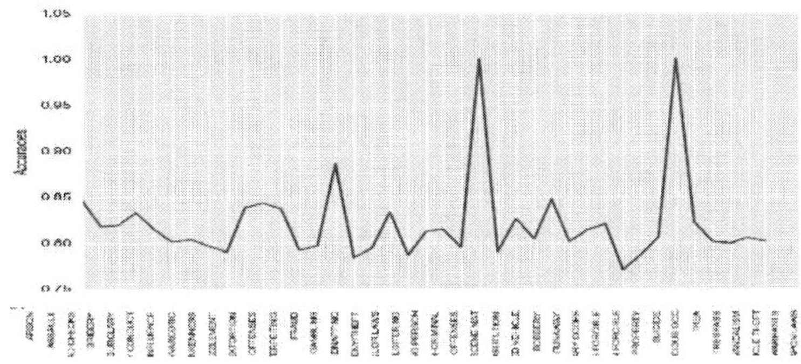

Fig. 2. Accuracy graph of naïve Bayes for all 39 categories of crime

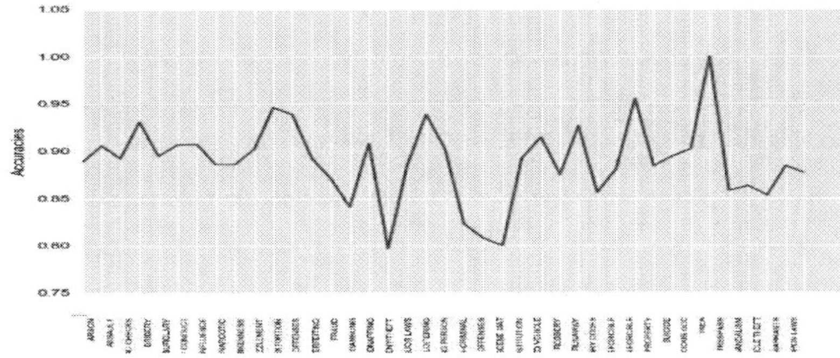

Fig. 3. Accuracy graph of random forest for all 39 categories of crime

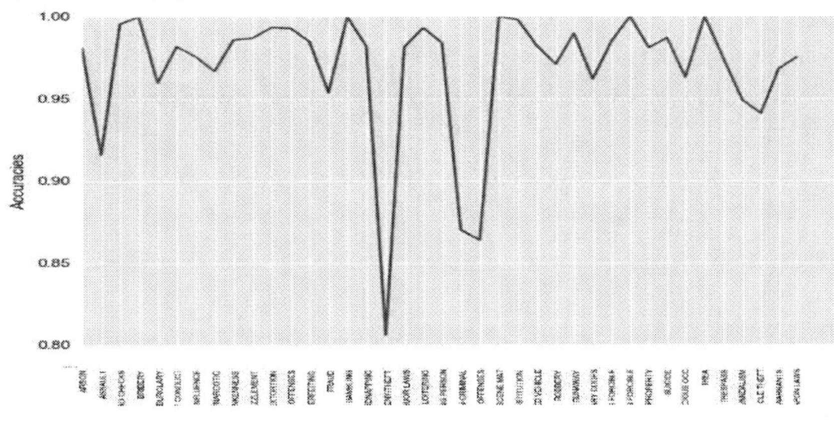

Fig. 4. Accuracy graph of SVM (RBF kernel) for all 39 categories of crime

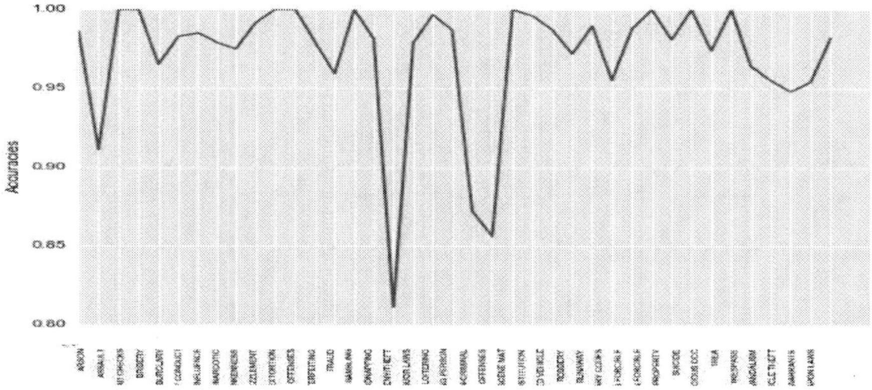

Fig. 5. Accuracy graph of SVM (linear kernel) for all 39 categories of crime

4.3. Graph of Predicted Probabilities of all Crime categories

After the user inputs the time frame and location, an algorithm is run to determine the probabilities of different crimes. These probabilities are compared to determine and predict the most probable crime for the given instance. These probabilities are analyzed through graphs shown from Fig. 6. to Fig. 10. The variations in the peaks, which indicates high probabilities, is very noticeable. The number of peaks have subsequently increased from decision tree to SVM.

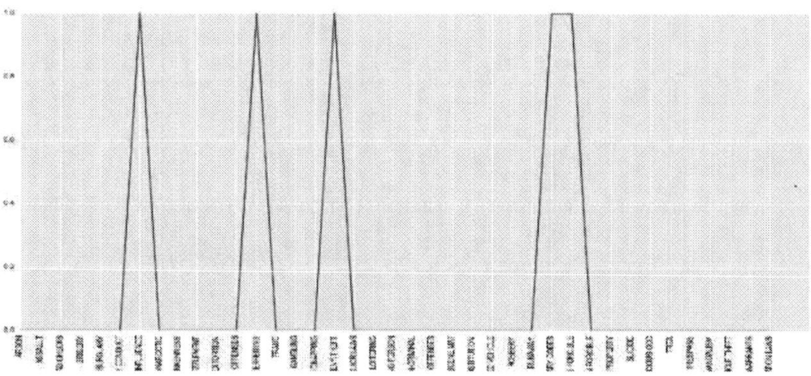

Fig. 6. Graph of predicted probabilities of all crime categories corresponding to a given user input (time stamp, location) using decision tree

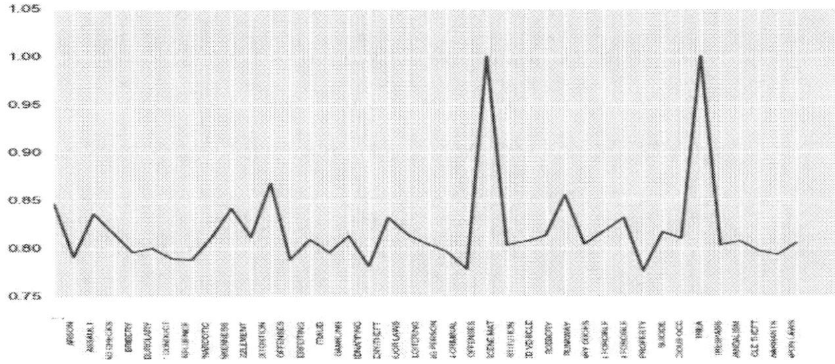

Fig. 7. Graph of predicted probabilities of all crime categories corresponding to a given user input (time stamp, location) using naïve Bayes

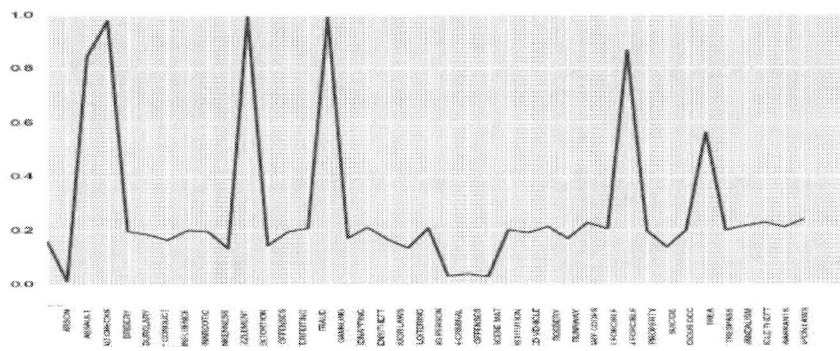

Fig. 8. Graph of predicted probabilities of all crime categories corresponding to a given user input (time stamp, location) using random forest .

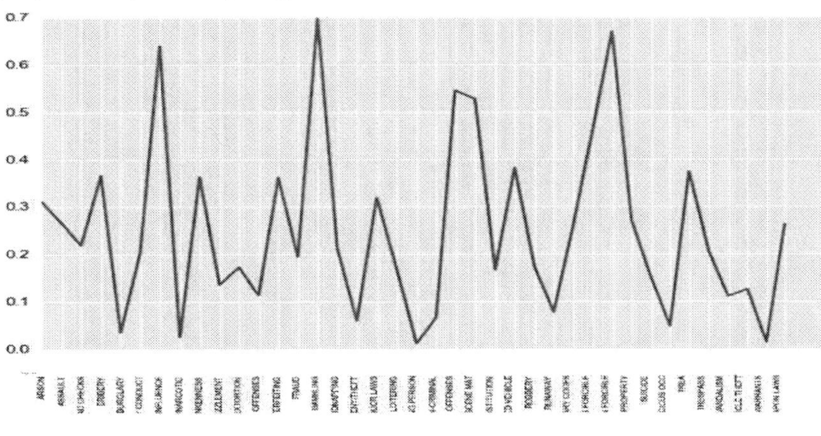

Fig. 9. Graph of predicted probabilities of all crime categories corresponding to a given user input (time stamp, location) using SVM (RBF kernel)

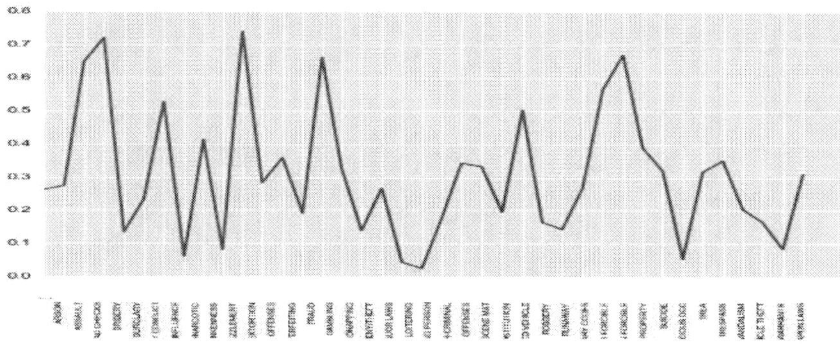

Fig. 10. Graph of predicted probabilities of all crime categories corresponding to a given user input (time stamp, location) using SVM (linear kernel)

4.4. Overall Accuracy

The average accuracies for the algorithms have been shown in Table **2**. Linear kernel SVM has the highest accuracy.

Table 2. Algorithms and their average accuracies

Algorithm	Average Accuracy
Decision Tree	80%
Naive Bayes	85%
Random Forest	85 - 89%
SVM (RBF kernel)	90%
SVM (linear kernel)	93%

Few other visualizations displaying the crime pattern have been done. One of which is shown in Fig. **11**. This figure shows the district-wise crime trends involving top ten crimes.

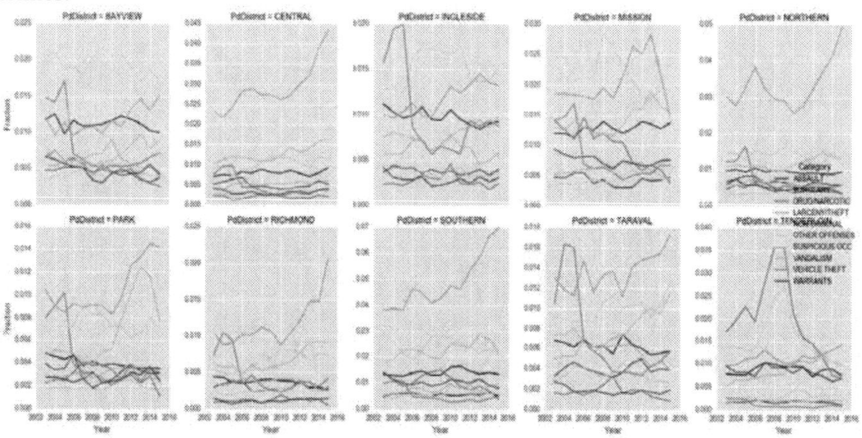

Fig. 11. District-wise crime trends concerning top ten crimes

4.1. Interactive San Francisco Map

Crime hot spots are shown in Fig. 12. The figure shows the map of San Francisco, crime categories on the right and a time filter. Two crimes, drug and prostitution are selected, along with this a time frame is selected. Crime hot spots corresponding to this instance are shown with separate color coding for the two crime categories.
Fig **13** shows a San Francisco map, where user can click to select a location, corresponding latitude and longitude is collected in the system, after this the user enters the date and time for which he wants to predict the data. It can be seen in the Python terminal that the predicted category of crime, Assault, is displayed in the end. The evaluation metrics for two crimes can also be seen, due to space constraints metrics for other crimes couldn't be shown here.

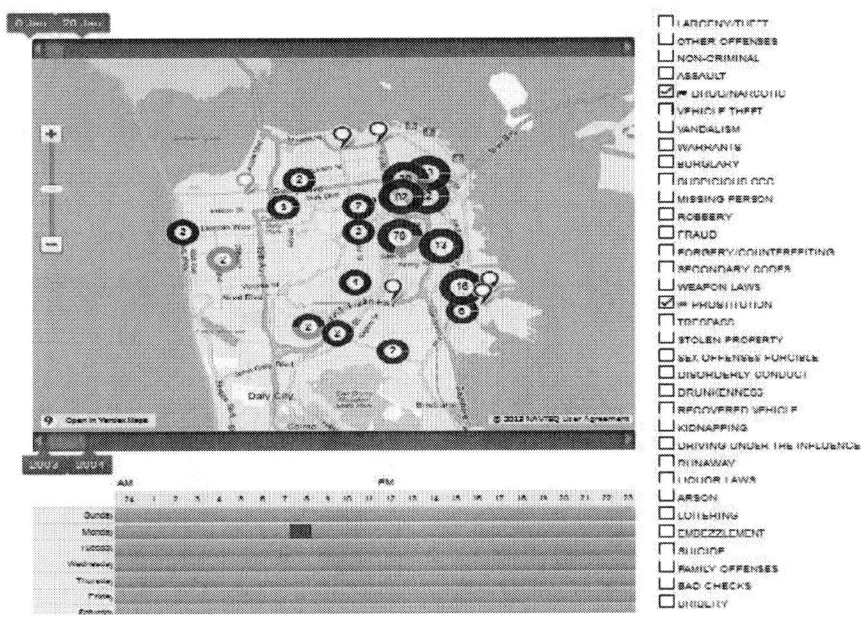

Fig. 12. Crime hot spots.

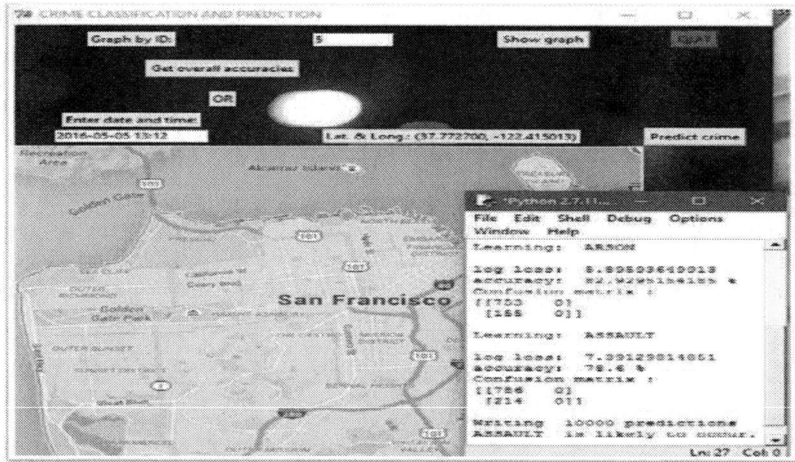

Fig. 13. Predicting the crime after manually selecting the location on map and entering the date and time in text field.

5. Conclusion and Future Enhancements

In this paper, machine learning techniques have been used to classify the category of crime and predict future occurrences of crime given demographics of place and time frame of crime.

Classifying 39 different types of crime categories is a perplexing multi-class classification problem. We have efficiently preprocessed the data and converted it into sparse matrix, considering the time and space constraints. We have compared and visualized the output of Decision tree, naïve Bayes, Random Forest and SVM. High accuracy up to 90% is achieved on using Random forest model and Support Vector Machines by training over past 12 years of data.

Few future enhancements that we think can be tried and incorporated to achieve an all-round improved performance are mentioned below:

- Exploring relationships between peaks of different categories of crimes – for example, if two or more classes of crimes surge and sink together, would be an interesting relationship to uncover.
- This system is limited to the San Francisco data sets, due to dataset availability issues. It can be expanded to other regions as well.
- Accepting other forms of raw data like textual data from news, social networks etc.

References

1. Hsinchun Chen, Wingyan Chung, Jennifer Jie Xu, Gang Wang, Yi Qin, Michael Chau (2004) Crime Data Mining: General Framework and some examlpes, IEEE computer society, vol. 37, no. 4, pp 50-56
2. Faisal Kamiran, Asim Karim, Sicco Verwer, Heike Goudriaan (2012), In: IEEE 12th International Conference on Data Mining Workshops, doi: DOI 10.1109/ICDMW.2012.117
3. Isuru Jayaweera, Chamath Sajeewa, Sampath, Liyanage, Tharindu Wijewardane, Indika Perera, Adeesha Wijayasiri (2015) Crime Analytics: Analysis of Crimes Through Newspaper Articles, IEEE computer society, vol. 42, pp 277-282
4. V. Nath (2006) Crime pattern detection using data mining, In: Web Intelligence and Intelligent Agent Technology Workshops, Hong Kong, pp 41-44
5. Jazeem Azeez, D. John Aravindhar (2015) Hybrid Approach to Crime Prediction using Deep learning, In: 2015 International Conference on Advances in Computing, Communications and Informatics (ICACCI), pp 1701-1710
6. Keivan Kianmehr (2006) Crime Hot-Spots Prediction Using Support Vector Machine, IEEE computer society
7. Kaggle Datasets, https://www.kaggle.com/datasets
8. Scikit-learn, http://scikit-learn.org/stable/
9. Tkinter, https://wiki.python.org/moin/TkInter

A Big Data Analytics Framework for Smart Grid Fault Prediction

Quang Nguyen, Bernardo Hermont, Sindhu Suresh

Siemens Corporate Technology, Princeton, NJ, USA
nguyen.quang@siemens.com
bernardo.hermont@siemens.com
sindhu.suresh@siemens.com

Abstract: Big Data Technologies have revolutionized many industries, such as web services (e.g. Google), social media (e.g. Facebook), retail (e.g. Amazon), etc. but there is a lack of application of Big Data in power and energy industry, especially in combination with Analytics and Machine Learning. Rapid deployment of intelligence devices within Smart Grids means huge amounts of data are collected every day from heterogeneous sources. Mining valuable insights from these data can bring big business values for energy industry. In this paper we describe an architecture where Big Data technologies can be utilized for Smart Grid applications, and a machine learning solution for a real world use case – fault prediction.

Keywords: Smart grid; analytics; big data; machine learning.

1. Introduction

Smart grid otherwise known as the future intelligent grid is the enhancement of the traditional grid in the 20th century. Transformation of the traditional grid to an intelligent grid which enables bidirectional flow is accomplished by the vast development in the field of sensor, information and communication technology. Smart grid, as the name indicates, makes the grid smarter to solve the variability created by the large penetration of renewable energy resources and the interaction of prosumer society. Smart grid could respond to events that occur anywhere in the grid starting from a consumer/prosumer node to a big generator. For instance, once a medium voltage transformer failure event occurs in the distribution grid, the smart grid may automatically change the power flow and recover the power delivery service [1]. This is possible because of the core technology development in the field of information technology, especially in the field of smart / big data.

Utilities used to store a vast amount of data (set points) which increased during the last 10 years with the development of more sensors in the network. Exponential increase in data calls for big data analytics. The information technology definition of big data is it is a collection of data sets so large and complex that it becomes difficult to process using on-hand database management tools or traditional data processing applications [2].

In this work we describe the general Big Data architecture that can be used for solving various use cases in Smart Grids, and specifically describe an analytics and machine learning solution for a real-world use case in Smart Grid – fault prediction.

2. Big Data for Smart Grids: Architecture and Technology Stack

In this section we describe the Big Data architecture and potential technologies to be used for our solution. Fehler! Verweisquelle konnte nicht gefunden werden. illustrates the proposed architecture, where the data flow through different layers: data sources, ingestion, processing, analytics and application. In the following subsection we discuss more details for each layer.

2.1. Data sources – Integration layer

The first layer in our Big Data architecture is Data Sources, or Integration layer, where data are collected from different entities in the Smart Grids: generation, transmission, distribution and consumer sources. Each data source typically has its own data management system, e.g. Cascade, PIMS, etc. which is designed to collected and manage data for its needs.

2.2. Ingestion Layer

This layer is responsible for ingesting data from different sources and put them in a storage space for analyzing in later steps. Data Lake, as shown in **Figure 1**, functions as such a storage space, where all (or almost all) of raw data from the sources are stored. Note that this architecture is built and used for not only one, but multiple use cases within a utility organization, and in practice use cases and data models are often not well-defined, or even not defined at all until the implementation phase. Therefore, data stored in the Data Lake typically keep the format from the source with very little (or none) transformation and filtering. In later steps of the pipeline these data will be filtered and transformed as needed, depending on the specific use cases.

The technology used for Data Lake is typically one that has scalability (easy to upgrade and maintain when data grows very fast in volume), reliability (e.g. prevent data loss through replication) and flexibility (store data in both structured and unstructured formats). Traditional relational database management systems, such as MS SQL Server or Oracle, have a number of limitations: typically they cannot run on commodity hardware; new nodes cannot be easily added (scaling out is a complex process in this case); there is limitations with regards to the number of nodes it can manage. Therefore, distributed data management systems like Hadoop or NoSQL databases (e.g. MongoDB) are preferable. With these systems, to expand storage capacity one just needs more (less-expensive) nodes to the existing set of nodes. This is economical and also does not cause down time of the system. Moreover, these systems are also designed to easily store huge amounts of data in its original, likely unstructured, format.

As mentioned in the previous section, each data source in Smart Grids may have its own data management system. Therefore, the ingestion tools to be used depend on the process being performed on the data. If it is just data movement, Sqoop or Nifi are probably the best options, but if there is need for transformation/aggregation, Talend, Pig, Informatica would be better choices.

2.3. Processing Layer

In this layer a sequence of ETL (Extraction, Transformation, Load) jobs can be implemented in order to extract and transform raw data in the Data Lake into data that is needed for analytics or end user applications. Data Warehouse and Operational Store may present in this layer, as shown in **Fehler! Verweisquelle konnte nicht gefunden werden**.

Data warehouse usually stores long term aggregated data to support historical analysis. Users will sometimes need highly aggregated data, and other times they will need to drill down to details. More sophisticated analyses include trend analyses and data mining, which use existing data to forecast trends or predict futures.

Operational data stores exist to support daily operations. In Operational Data Store (ODS) data is cleaned and validated, but it is not historically deep: it may be just the data for the current day. Rather than support the historically rich queries that a data warehouse can handle, the ODS gives data warehouses a place to get access to the most current data, which has not yet been loaded into the data warehouse. The ODS may also be used as a source to load the data warehouse.

Data warehouse and ODS usually require fast and frequent access to data, so typically a relational DB, such as MS SQL or Teradata DB, is used for this purpose. Sometimes, NoSQL DB, e.g. MongoDB, can be used for, but only if the end user application does not perform random access to the DB frequently, e.g. usually only loads a big chunk of data without searching for specific data items.

For processing purposes one can use any tool that provides an access interface to the underlying storage system. For example, Talend can access and process data in both Hadoop and NoSQL DB (e.g. MongoDB).

3.4. Analytics Layer

This is the layer where analytics workflows analyze data, learn insights and patterns from the data and produce analytics results. Different analytics tools and data mining algorithms can be used here, depending on the use case. For example, tools like R, Python, Mahout and Spark provide a rich set of data mining and machine learning algorithms, e.g. classification, regression, clustering, principal component analysis, etc. Knime is another tool that provides a visual workflow management interface, that help to connect and manage many data mining algorithms.

3.5. Application Layer

This layer contains user applications that utilize the outputs produced by the processing and/or analytics layer. Examples of such applications are those that visualize data, report useful statistics, or take some actions to response to the analytics results (e.g. send alerts to users).

4. An Use Case of Analytics for Smart Grids: Fault Prediction

In this section we propose an analytics approach and machine learning algorithm for the use case of fault detection. The goal is to predict a failure of an electric equipment (feeder, transformer, etc.) before it happens.

4.1. Analytics Approach

This section describes a machine learning approach to predict permanent failures of equipment in Smart Grid (e.g. a feeder) based on the time series of voltage and current recorded by sensors and history of failures.

Given a time series, the goal is to be able to predict a (permanent) failure before it happens, $\boldsymbol{k}$ hours in advance, i.e. if a failure happens at time $\boldsymbol{t}$, we want to predict it at time $\boldsymbol{t - k}$. We first find all failure events of this equipment that happened in our historical data, then for each time point when a failure happens, e.g. time $\boldsymbol{t}$, we analyze data in a time window of $\boldsymbol{n}$ hours from $\boldsymbol{t - k - n}$ to $\boldsymbol{t - k}$ to find the patterns that are indicative / predictive of the failure. For example, a failure happened at 6pm, December 15, and we want to predict the failure 2 hours in advance, e.g. at 4pm, we can analyze time series recorded in the time window of n = 3 hours from 1pm to 4pm (as shown in Figure **1**).

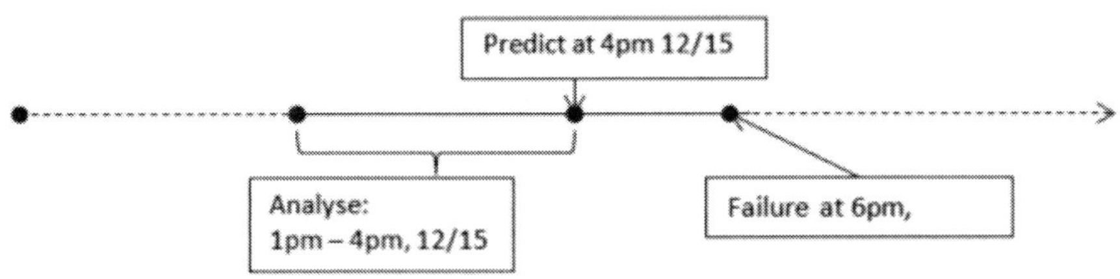

Figure 1. Timeline for the period of data analysis, prediction and failure

Within the analyzed time window we perform *Discrete Wavelet Transformation (DWT)* [3] to transform the fraction of time series (in that time window) into a vector of features. This vector of features would serve as a "failure" training example. Further in this document these will be called *"positive examples"*, as a widely accepted terminology in data mining / machine learning field.

Now we need to formulate "normal operating" training examples so that our learning algorithm can learn to distinguish them from "failure" examples. For this exercise we examine history of normal operating periods when no failure happened. Then we can sample a set of n-hours, e.g. 3-hour windows from these periods; perform Discrete Wavelet Transformation on the sub - time series to transform them into vectors of features. These vectors form the "normal operating" training examples. Further in this document these will be called *"negative examples"*, as a widely accepted terminology in data mining / machine learning field.

Since the time series could be very long the dimension of feature vectors after DWT could be very high (if there are 128 samples per second => ~ 1.38 M per 3-hour window). Therefore we need to do *dimensionality reduction* to transform feature vectors into vectors of lower (< 100) dimension. This can be done by using different techniques such as Principal Component Analysis (PCA) [5] or singular value decomposition (SVD) [6].

Given the set of positive and negative examples in lower dimension, we can use classification machine learning algorithms such as Decision Trees [7], Support Vector Machines (SVM) [8], Logistic Regression [9] or Neural Networks [10] to learn the predictive model.

Training data is represented in the form of a table (matrix) of M rows and N columns, where each column represents a data feature (result of DWT transformation on original time series), and each row represents a vector of feature values for a specific time window. Training labels (or targets) are represented in the form of a vector of M elements where each element is a training target value (failure or not) at a specific time point.

For constructing features we used time series related to the equipment (e.g. feeder, substation, etc.): Voltage (V), Current (A), Real power (W), Reactive power (VAR) and time series of weather data: Temperature (deg F), Wind speed (mph).

4.2. Algorithm Pseudocode

In this section we provide pseudocode for the analytics solution described in the previous section. The pseudocode will produce a training model as the output, which later can be applied to future data for failure prediction.

function ***fault_prediction***

input:

- o k – number of hours before a failure that the prediction needs to be made
- o n – length of time window to be analyzed
- o Data set TF which contains failure history
- o Data set TN which contains normal operating history
- o Data sets D_1, D_2, ... D_n where each D_i is a data set containing time series of voltage, current, power, etc.
- o Data set D_weather contains weather data

output: model = weight vector (w_1, w_2, ..., w_m), where m is the total number of features extracted from D_1, D_2, ..., D_n

```
        initialize matrix X = {}, vector y = {}
        // matrix X represents training data matrix, initially is empty; vector y represents
        training targets, initially empty

        // create positive examples
        for each failure time point t_i in TF
            for each D_i, i=1..n do
                filtered_D_i = filter_data_in_time_window (startTime = t_i-k -n, end-
                Time = t_i-k )
                matrix X_i = feature_engineer (data_set = filtered_D_i)
                X = combine(X,X_i)          //X_i is gradually added (concatenated col-
                umn-wise) to X
                y = combine(y,1)  // a positive label "1" is added to y
            end
        end

        //create negative examples
        TS = sample (TN)    //sample a set of n-hour time windows from normal operating
        data
        for each time window (start,end)_i in TS
            for each D_i, i=1..n do
            filtered_D_i = filter_data_in_time_window (startTime = start_i, endTime = end_i)
            matrix X_i = feature_engineer (data_set = filtered_D_i)
            X = combine(X,X_i)          // X_i is gradually added (concatenated column-wise)
            to X
            y = combine(y,0) // a negative label "0" is added to y
            end
        end

        X' = dimensionality_reduction(X)        // use principal component analysis (PCA)
        or singular value decomposition (SVD)
        X_weather = feature_engineer (data_set = D_weather)
        //note that weather in a short time window is likely not high dimensional, so we
        may not need to do dimensionality reduction for weather related features
        train_X = combine(X', X_weather)
        vector w = train_model(y, train_X, classification_method) //launching function to
        learn the model
        return w
end

// function train_model learns a predictive model, input is a target value vector y, a data
matrix X, and regression type; output is a weight vector w
function train_model(y, X, classification_method)
        switch classification_method
                //function to perform Support Vector Machines on X and y
                case "SVM": w = SVM(y, X, svm_parameters)
                //function to perform DecisionTree on X and y
                case "DecisionTree": w = DecisionTree(y, X, tree_parameters)
                    //function to perform Logistic Regression
```

```
        case "LogisticRegression": w = LogisticRegression(y, X, regres-
        sion_parameters)
        //function to perform Neural Network
        case "NeuralNet": w = NeuralNet(y, X, neuralNet_parameters)
    end
return w
end
```

5. Conclusion

Big Data and machine learning technologies have been proved to bring huge values in many industries, such as e-commerce, social networks, financial services, etc. However, the power of these technologies has not been utilized fully in energy industry. In this work we describe a solution architecture that incorporates various big data technologies and a machine learning algorithm to solve a use case in energy industry – fault prediction. While the machine learning algorithm is tailored for this use case, the big data architecture can be generalized to solve various use cases where the solution depends on the analysis of large amounts of data. These use cases, e.g. asset management, smart grid load/price forecast, energy trading, etc. have been increasingly common in energy industry nowadays due to the wide adoption of smart meters and network sensors.

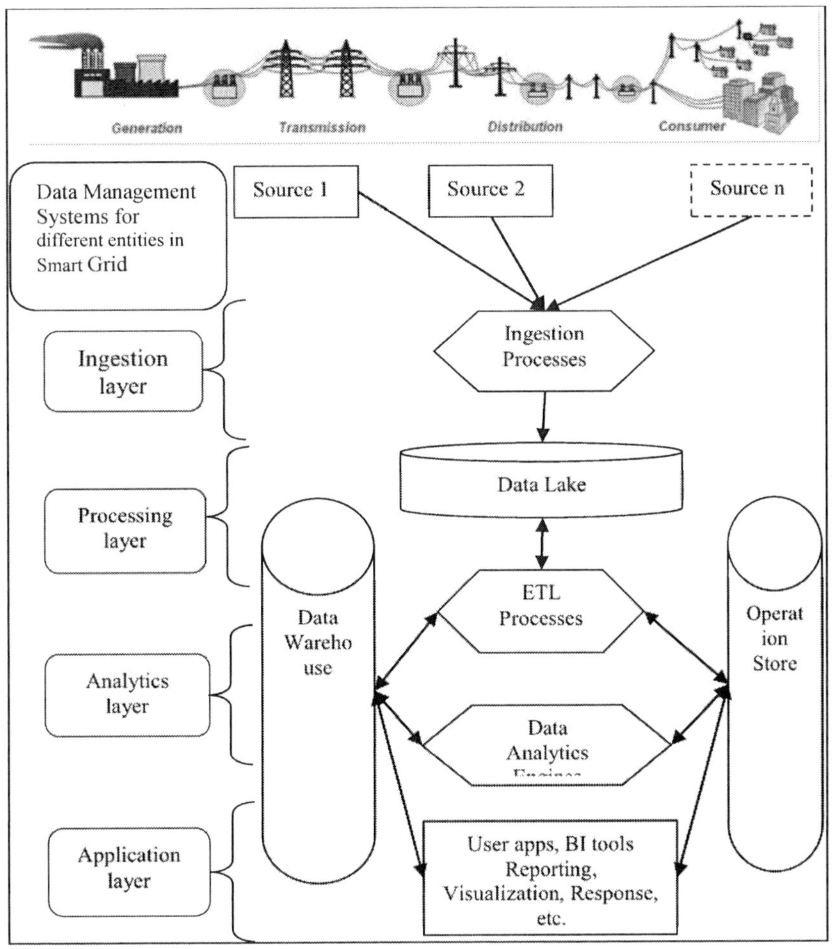

Figure 2. Big Data Architecture for Smart Grids.

References

1. Xi Fang, Satyajayant Misra, Guoliang Xue, Dejun Yang. Smart Grid – The New and Improved Power Grid: A Survey. IEEE Communications Surveys & Tutorials (Volume: 14, Issue: 4, Fourth Quarter 2012).
2. Stanley E. McHann Jr. Grid Analytics: How Much Data Do You Really Need? Rural Electric Power Conference (REPC), 2013.
3. Ingrid Daubechies. Orthonormal bases of compactly supported wavelets. Communications on Pure and Applied Mathematics (November, 1988) 909–996.

4. Fodor,I. (2002) "A survey of dimension reduction techniques". Center for Applied Scientific Computing, Lawrence Livermore National, Technical Report UCRL-ID-148494
5. Jolliffe I.T. Principal Component Analysis, Series: Springer Series in Statistics, 2nd ed., Springer, NY, 2002, XXIX, 487 p. 28 illus. ISBN 978-0-387-95442-4
6. Golub, G. H.; Reinsch, C. (1970). Singular value decomposition and least squares solutions. Numerische Mathematik. 14 (5): 403–420. doi:10.1007/ BF02163027. MR 1553974
7. Breiman, Leo; Friedman, J. H.; Olshen, R. A.; Stone, C. J. (1984). Classification and regression trees. Monterey, CA: Wadsworth & Brooks/Cole Advanced Books & Software. ISBN 978-0-412-04841-8
8. Cortes, C.; Vapnik, V. (1995). "Support-vector networks". Machine Learning. 20 (3): 273–297. doi:10.1007/BF00994018
9. Cox, DR (1958). The regression analysis of binary sequences (with discussion). J Roy Stat Soc B. 20: 215–242.
10. Rumelhart, D.E; James McClelland (1986). Parallel Distributed Processing: Explorations in the Microstructure of Cognition. Cambridge: MIT Press.

Simulation based Approach for Special Discounting Threshold

Shashank Shekhar, Kaushik Shankar, Bishwarup Bhattacharjee, Sushanta Kumar Mishra, Sam Pritchett, and Parag Chitalia

VMware Inc., Palo Alto, USA
sshekhar@vmware.com; shankark@vmware.com; bbhattacharj@vmware.com; skumarmishra@vmware.com; spritchett@vmware.com; pchitalia@vmware.com

Abstract: There are many existing solutions available that provide a recommendation to increase the threshold of the minimum order size to avail special discounts (SPF) by minimizing the loss in order conversion. The goal of such solutions is to maximize the earning and maximize quote to order conversion. However, these solutions are primarily based on relationship between order size and quote to order conversion and utilize historical conversion rates at different price points (List price-Discount). This paper illustrates the use of Single Item Single Period Newsvendor problem and Extreme Gradient Tree Boosting methods to simulate a case for increasing order thresholds and calculating the corresponding loss in order conversion. The boosting method was applied on the training data and simulated and cross validated across three test data sets to test three different price change scenarios. We compute the expected quotes at the end of the period and expected conversion at the end of the period to maximize profit.

Keywords: Extreme Gradient Tree Boosting, SPF, List Price, B2B, Single Item Single Period Newsvendor problem, quotes, conversion.

1. Introduction

VMware (VMW) is a virtualization, end user computing and cloud company with annual revenues of USD 7 BB (as of 2016) and a market cap of USD 38 BB [1]. Total revenue is comprised of license revenue of $2,794 million and services revenue of $4,299 million. VMware sells products in the Software Defined Data Center (vSphere, VSAN, NSX for computing, storage & network virtualization respectively), end user computing (Airwatch, Horizon, and Fusion/Workstation) and cloud. These are all sold to B2B customers.

The prices of products at VMW have been rarely changed over time [2]. However Sales reps could offer discounts *via* SPF flag which is a special discretionary discount which should ideally be given for large orders. The Pricing Business Unit was keen to figure out a way to get to optimal list prices at VMW. Sometimes order quotes are drafted using a Special Pricing Form (SPF). Typically, large order sizes qualify under SPF quotes. The sales reps provide a discount to the customer for such orders called as SPF discount. The paper focusses on building a case for increasing SPF order size thresholds from the current value to a higher value (50% increment/100% incre-

ment/150% increment). The goal of the business was to reduce costs by reducing the number of SPF orders thereby maximize profit and evaluate the potential risks associated with it.
We attempt to determine the optimum threshold for the Special Pricing orders by lowering the discount value. Here, discount rate is used as a proxy for order size threshold. Lowering the discount will lead to a higher order price which results in a higher threshold. Instead of analyzing the quotes in a descriptive manner, here we focus on developing a predictive model and simulate what-if scenarios for different SPF thresholds.

2. Solution Framework

2.1. Objectives

The Advanced Analytics & Data Sciences team came up with the following objectives with the Pricing Business Unit.

- Analyze historical SPF data/price & discount trends/order conversions
- Identify significant drivers of SPF order conversion
- Compute expected quotes (demand) and expected conversion at the end of the period
- Build a model to determine optimum deal size in order to qualify for a SPF transaction.

2.2. Strategy

A traditional discounting optimization problem would use order conversion based on discounts given on different deal size. But since the threshold for SPF discount was fixed, the data did not indicate the probability of order conversion for an increased threshold. The data was simulated to get non-SPF discount for quotes which qualified for SPF discounts and then the probability of quote to order conversion was computed. The trend of SPF discounts was visualized using quote to order matching method. This included product-specific weighted discounting patterns, GEO/Region patterns, seasonality analysis, reason code, etc. and also included assessing if List Prices are within acceptable ranges (e.g. are we using SPF more because of high list price?)

SPF requests are useful indicators to infer the customer's assignment of value to a product. SPF flag is a discount that can be given by a sales representative on request – mostly given on large order sizes. An increase in threshold of minimum order size for SPF discount can potentially lead into non-conversion of the order and hence can result in revenue loss for VMware, Inc. The intent of the project was to determine optimum threshold such that the increase in overall price offsets the revenue loss due to decrease in conversion, thereby maximizing the overall profit. Following detailed steps were planned:

- Determine magnitude of SPF orders and their impact on overall revenue
- Visualize the trends of SPFs by type using quote to order matching method

- Compute expected deals won/lost using Single Item Single Period Newsvendor problem [3]
- Identify drivers of discounting behaviors
- Recommend policy changes supported by findings

2.3. Solution Approach

Objective was to determine the magnitude of increment in minimum order size for SPF discounting which results in minimum loss in conversion. There was a need to create a base set of research data (Customer -> Approved Quotes -> Order) which needed to be standardized and approved to be used for modelling. Exploratory data analyses were done to depict a relationship between amount of discount and actual bookings. The analyses show GEO level differences in behavior patterns. Clustering was done on the behavior patterns and the clusters were aligned to decision tree [4] output to determine drivers of outliers.

The estimation of expected quotes and conversion gave us an indication of proportion of win/loss in different scenarios. The modeling was done to estimate the proportion of win/loss for different order size threshold. The final recommendation was the new threshold based on conversion probability for each evaluated threshold.

3. Modeling

3.1. Dataset Creation

The data matrix for the model was aggregated at an order-SKU level using Greenplum and Hadoop. This is because our entity is the combination of an order and a SKU. Specific business level judgements were applied like:

- Dataset for a time period of FY14Q1 to FY16Q4
- Specific products like vCloud Air that had a subscription model/enterprise license agreements (ELAs) that have pre-determined prices transactions were removed while creating this dataset
- Given large amounts of data, the data was picked from Hadoop, where we took last 5 years of dataset related to site made available by IT in a flat tabular structure at order-SKU level.
- The continuous variables were subjected to coarse classing and fine classing depending on nature of variable to arrive at bins which can be used as an input to the model.
- Opportunity data was added to the dataset to include the following:
    - Time from Opportunity to Quote
    - Time from Quote to Conversion
    - Outliers where a quote is generated after the Opportunity Close date
- The key independent variables were Quote Value, Total Deal Score, Product platform, SPF deal size, industry vertical, sales classification etc.

- The dependent variables was a bookings flag which indicated quote to order conversion

3.2. Estimation of expected profit based on Deals Won/Lost

We used part of Single Item Single Period Newsvendor problem to estimate the numbers of deals won/lost at the end of a period to give an indication of net change in revenue.

Let;

p = List Price per unit

i = Invoice price per unit

r = rebate/discounts other than SPF per unit per period ($ per unit per period)

s = SPF discount in $ per unit

k = Incremental revenue due to change in threshold deal size for SPF discount

Q = quantity sold (no. of units)

x = demand per period (No. of quotes per period); stochastic with F(x) as the cumulative distribution of total demand and f(x) as the probability distribution function

π = Incremental profit

Let $\mu = E[x]$ be the expected demand per period

Let I(Q) = Expected deals won at the end of the period

Let B(Q) = Expected deals lost at the end of the period

$$I(Q) = \int_0^Q (x - Q)f(x)dx \ (continuous\ demand);\ I(Q) = \sum_0^Q (x - Q)f(x)(discrete\ demand) \quad (1)$$

$$B(Q) = \int_Q^\infty (x - Q)f(x)dx \ (continuous\ demand);\ B(Q) = \sum_{Q+1}^\infty (x - Q)f(x)(discrete\ demand) \quad (2)$$

It can be shown that

$$B'(x) = F(x)-1 \quad (3)$$

$$I'(x) = F(x) \quad (4)$$

For discrete demand it can be shown that $\Delta\{\sum_{Q+1}^{\infty}(x - Q)f(x)\}$ =F(Q)-1 where $\Delta\{f(r)\} = f(r) - f(r-1)$ (5)

Expected Incremental Profit = E[π] = Expected Revenue – Standard Rebate/Discount – SPF Discount + Incremental Revenue due to change in SPF threshold (6)

$$E[\pi(Q)] = E[\min(Q,x)]*p - r*I(Q) - s*I(Q) + K*I(Q) \quad (7)$$

It can be shown that maximizing expected profit is same as minimizing the number of deals lost (in-turn maximizing the number of deals won) due to increase in threshold deal size for SPF discount.

3.3. Model for Quote to Order Conversion

For the model, the target variable is a booking flag that indicates whether a quote is converted given that the quote is approved. It makes sense to only consider approved quotes in this regard, as a quote has nil probability of being converted if it is not approved by VMWare. We also confine ourselves to a very granular level of data to provide robustness to our model. Below we describe the filters we applied to our training data:

- We considered only the quotes located in AMER region.
- We only consider quotes that contain at least one licensed products.
- We only consider standard form of SPF and exclude quotes where blanket or recurring SPF were applied.
- We also remove all the quotes containing AirWatch products (MOBILE-EMM-EMM).

Our modelling approach is driven by the idea to explore the fact that had we offered non-SPF discount on the same set of quotes, then what would possibly have happened in terms of probability of conversion.

Assuming that the current order size threshold for SPF discount is $X, we derived five deal size buckets, which are:

- < $ X
- $ X – $ 1.5X
- $ 1.5X - $ 2X
- $ 2X - $ 2.5X
- > $ 2.5X

For each of the above deal size buckets we obtained the historical discounts given to quotes belonging to both SPF and non-SPF, we trained an Extreme Gradient Boosting (xGBoost) [5] model on the filtered data. We score our models based on a 4-fold cross-validation and selection evaluation criteria as the area under the ROC curve (AUC) [6]. We considered different hyper-parameter combinations and chose the best model offering the best out-of-fold estimate (around 0.7).

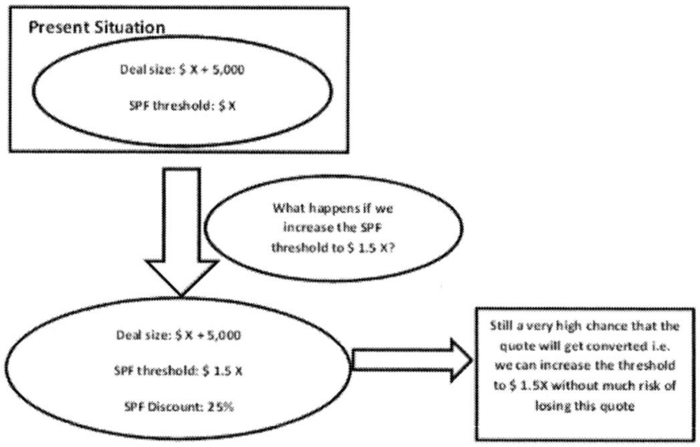

Figure 1. Current and Proposed Scenarios.

For the test data, we created three different data sets – by keeping all other variables as is in the train data but changing the discount to non-SPF average discount in the respective buckets.

Table 1. Test Dataset 1: SPF threshold $ 1.5X (X = Current SPF threshold)

Deal Size	Discount Type
Less than $ X	Non-SPF
Between $ X and $ 1.5X	Non-SPF
Between $ 1.5X and $ 2X	SPF
Between $ 2X and $ 2.5X	SPF
Greater than $ 2.5X	SPF

Table 2. Test Dataset 1: SPF threshold $ 2X (X = Current SPF threshold)

Deal Size	Discount Type
Less than $ X	Non-SPF
Between $ X and $ 1.5X	Non-SPF
Between $ 1.5X and $ 2X	Non-SPF
Between $ 2X and $ 2.5X	SPF
Greater than $ 2.5X	SPF

Table 3. Test Dataset 1: SPF threshold $ 2.5X (X = Current SPF threshold)

Deal Size	Discount Type
Less than $ X	Non-SPF
Between $ X and $ 1.5X	Non-SPF
Between $ 1.5X and $ 2X	Non-SPF
Between $ 2X and $ 2.5X	Non-SPF
Greater than $ 2.5X	SPF

For each of the test sets we obtained the probability of conversion in each of the buckets. To compare the simulated situations in test sets and the present discounting situation, we evaluated the mean conversion rate in each of the above five buckets result of which are shown in the tables below:

Table 4. Mock-up representation of Deals Lost for Deal Size threshold $ 1.5X (X = Current SPF threshold)

Deal Size Bucket`	Total Deals	Percentage Conversion Before	Percentage Conversion After	Deals Lost
≥ $ 2.5X	13642	0.201%	0.201%	0
$ 2X - $ 2.5X	1535	0.244%	0.244%	0
$ 1.5X - $ 2X	2034	0.268%	0.268%	0
$ X - $ 1.5 X	2393	0.276%	0.273%	7
< $ X	2166	0.31%	0.31%	0

The model indicated significantly low decrement in order conversion for a 50% increase in deal size threshold. The deal size bucket $ X - $ 1.5X is the only bucket affected by the proposed increase in the deal size threshold.

Similar evaluation was done for scenarios where threshold deal size were increased to $ 2X and $ 2.5X. The difference between the incremental revenue generated by the won deals and the revenue lost due to lost deals was computed.

Table 5. Mock-up representation of Deals Lost for Deal Size threshold $ 2X (X = Current SPF threshold)

Deal Size Bucket`	Total Deals	Percentage Conversion Before	Percentage Conversion After	Deals Lost
≥ $ 2.5X	13642	0.201%	0.201%	0
$ 2X - $ 2.5X	1535	0.244%	0.244%	0
$ 1.5X - $ 2X	2034	0.268%	0.208%	121
$ X - $ 1.5 X	2393	0.276%	0.273%	7
< $ X	2166	0.31%	0.31%	0

Table 6. Mock-up representation of Deals Lost for Deal Size threshold $ 2.5X (X = Current SPF threshold)

Deal Size Bucket	Total Deals	Percentage Conversion Before	Percentage Conversion After	Deals Lost
≥ $ 2.5X	13642	0.201%	0.201%	0
$ 2X - $ 2.5X	1535	0.244%	0.188%	80
$ 1.5X - $ 2X	2034	0.268%	0.208%	121
$ X - $ 1.5 X	2393	0.276%	0.273%	7
< $ X	2166	0.31%	0.31%	0

3.4. Determining Relative Importance of drivers of Discount

The relative importance of the factors influencing SPF discounts were determined by running Gradient Boosting Model [7]. The target variable for finding the relative importance of driver was Perpetual Blended Discount. The measures are based on the number of times a variable is selected for splitting, weighted by the squared improvement to the model as a result of each split, and averaged over all trees. Here we fit multiple trees in each stage in a one-vs-all way.

4. Conclusion

The solution provided for optimizing the order size threshold for SPF discounting VMware Inc. is unique and distinctive because the thresholds have been constant since inception and there have been hardly any instance of changing the threshold. The estimation of expected incremental profit based on deals won/lost after changing the SPF threshold is industry-first and there is no existing solution which does that. Also, the implemented approach was very different from standard optimization methodologies where historical changes are utilized to arrive at recommended price changes. From an algorithmic perspective, the approach is unique and there is no such implementation that utilizes simulation and boosting technique to arrive at threshold which maximizes profitability.

The recommendation to increase the order size threshold for ~60% of the SKUs was given to the business. It was also recommended to increase the threshold in phased manner and actively track the quote to order conversion. SPF usage is an indicator of customers' perception to extended list price and hence the recommendation was to make the change independent of other changes and to keep the standard rebate/discount constant as earlier. This will enable us to directly measure customers' perception to value. The recommendations from this project will help maximize profit for VMware, Inc. and also actively track price perception.

References

1. VMware Inc. Annual Report, http://ir.vmware.com/annuals.cfm
2. Rama K. *et al.* (2016) List Price Optimization Using Customized Decision Trees. In: Perner P. (eds) Machine Learning and Data Mining in Pattern Recognition. Lecture Notes in Computer Science, vol 9729. Springer, Cham
3. Gallego G, Moon I. The distribution free newsboy problem: review and extensions. J Opl Res Soc 1993;44:825- 34
4. Quinlan, J. R., (1986). Induction of Decision Trees. Machine Learning 1: 81-106, Kluwer Academic Publishers
5. Tianqi Chen, Carlos Guestrin (March 2016) XGBoost: A Scalable Tree Boosting System. https://arxiv.org/abs/1603.02754 [cs.LG]
6. Xavier RobinEmail , Natacha Turck, Alexandre Hainard, Natalia Tiberti, Frédérique Lisacek, Jean-Charles Sanchez and Markus Mülle (March 2011). pROC: an open-source package for R and S+ to analyze and compare ROC curves
7. Jerome H. Friedman Stochastic gradient boosting; Computational Statistics & Data Analysis Volume 38, Issue 4, 28 February 2002, Pages 367–378
8. M Dowle, A Srinivasan, T Short, S Lianoglou with contributions from R Saporta, E Antonyan https://cran.r-project.org/web/packages/data.table/data.table.pdf (PDF)
9. Hastie, T., Tibshirani, R., Friedman, J. H. (2001). The elements of statistical learning: Data mining, inference, and prediction. New York: Springer Verlag
10. Breiman, Leo; Friedman, J. H.; Olshen, R. A.; Stone, C. J. (1984). Classification and Regression trees. Monterey, CA: Wadsworth & Brooks/Cole Advanced Books & Software. ISBN 978-0-412-04841-8
11. Cohen, J., Cohen P., West, S.G., & Aiken, L.S. (2003). Applied multiple regression/correlation analysis for the behavioral sciences. (2nd ed.) Hillsdale, NJ: Lawrence Erlbaum Associates

Geographic Named Entity Recognition in Twitter

LaKeisha Williams[1], Sarah Darley[2,*], Lucas A. Overbey[1], and Scott C. Batson[1]

[1]Space and Naval Warfare Systems Center Atlantic P.O. Box 190022
North Charleston, SC 29419-9022
[2]University of South Carolina Computer Science and Engineering Department,
315 Main Street Columbia, SC 29208

Abstract. During emergencies, the volume of information produced via social media sites, like Twitter, increases rapidly. Much of this information is not useful; however, many messages still provide critical information to emergency responders. Effectively extracting this information from the noise is very challenging. One strategy to filter social media data and ensure that useful information is prioritized in a region affected by an emergency or natural disaster is to find reports that are the most geographically pertinent. Identifying geographic terms that provide this information from text could provide first responders with such regionally relevant information. The approach covered in this research involves using Natural Language Processing (NLP) techniques to extract highly specific named entities from social media data. Most Named Entity Recognition (NER) systems are trained on highly grammatical text and their performance significantly degrades in domains with specialized structure and syntax. In addition, the extracted entities may reveal locations but do not achieve the granularity necessary to automatically identify whether a discovered location is a street, city, country, or landmark. In order to handle the non-standard syntax of Twitter, we trained a Conditional Random Field (CRF) NER model on emergency management (EM) related Twitter data from users in Australia and Canada. The model utilizes a finely-grained focus on specific location-based information. The resulting NER model shows improved results on Twitter-specific data associated with emergency management information and can extract more specific details about location information than other NER CRF models.

Keywords: geographic, named entity recognition, social media, natural language processing, Twitter, emergency response, conditional random field.

1 Introduction

This research project stemmed from a project involving the geographic profiling of social media [1]. Social Media Geographic Profiling (SMGP) project uses Twitter messages as the primary source for text data. Twitter consists of very brief, unstructured, infrequent blocks of text commonly referred to as tweets. The Named Entity Recognition (NER) approach is being tested to make an attempt at improving the classification of entities, specifically geographic entities, from Twitter messages by analyzing message content that references physical locations.

NER is an information extraction task stemming from natural language processing (NLP) that attempts to locate and categorize entities within blocks of text. NER uses a combination of statistical models and grammar-based techniques trained to identify types of entities such as names of persons, organizations, locations, expressions of times, quantities, etc. NER systems are often domain specific, thus the reason to train the system for the domain in which it is intended to be used. NER models trained on traditional media produce poor results when used to filter data from social media sites such as Twitter, so the goal of this project is to train a new NER model using Stanford's open-source NER system and domain-specific data from Twitter that is tagged with the relevant entities.

Challenges identified when testing NER systems on Twitter data are the use of slang terms, little or no punctuation, text abbreviations (e.g. LOL, idk, brb, etc.), and messaging shortcuts. Traditionally, NER relies on capitalization of words in text as an indication of the existence of an entity. Tweets may not contain capitalization but may reference named entities thus presenting another problem with using a traditional NER system. After analyzing the text content in tweets with regard to geographic or physical location, it was determined that certain phrasal or context words contribute to the possible identification of geographic/location-based entities. This provided an opportunity to use the context and phrases to enhance the NER systems tested in addition to combining this technique with other statistical and text similarity scores.

2 Approach

We wanted to train the model to recognize locations within Twitter data. Considering the geographic nature of the research within emergency management (EM), the data collection began with a search of Australian and Canadian organizations with a Twitter presence in either emergency management, police, fire, weather, or news. The data was extracted from Twitter using the Australian and Canadian-based user accounts via the Twitter API. The program collected tweets and some additional metadata from these accounts. Consideration was given to the number of tweets necessary to train and test the model. Of the tweets collected, a total of 20,000 tweets were randomly selected to be used to train the model. 14,000 of these tweets were used to train the NER model, while the remaining 6,000 tweets were used to test the results of the trained model.

2.1 Data Extraction and Cleaning

The data was cleaned to account for the various issues associated with text data obtained from Twitter. The cleaning process involved removing web links and special characters such as:

- Comma: “ , ”
- Period: “ . ”
- Exclamation: “ ! ”
- Asterisk: “ * ”
- Question: “ ? ”

These characters were found unnecessary to the relevance of preparing the data for tokenization and model training. The special characters kept were those characters such as:

- Underscore: “ ”
- Dash: “ -”
- Semicolon: “ ; ”
- Forward Slash: “ / ”
- Hashtag: “ # ”
- Colon: “ : ”
- At sign: “ @ ”

The characters # and @ are commonly used in Twitter and refer to the usernames and hashtags within the geographic NER model. The @ sign is also often used to specify "at" a location. These special characters assist in providing context to the text within the tweet data.
Capitalization is often used in many NER systems to identify named entities. However, in Twitter many named entities and words are not capitalized so capitalization was removed from each word prior to tokenization.

2.2 Data Tagging

First, in order to train a model, the team tagged the Twitter data specific to the domain in which we were interested for this study. A preprocessing step of tokenizing the data was completed prior to tagging. The tagging process required that each token in the training and testing files be labeled with the appropriate entity. The entities used for tagging: PERSON, DIRECTION, ORGANIZATION, DATE, TIME, EVENT, LOC STREET, LOC CITY, LOC STATE, LOC COUNTRY, and LOC MISC.
These entities are geographically focused, but include other information that could be relevant to determining identity and location as well. The tagging process was partially automated using a program and dictionary files for common occurrences in the domain dataset such as hashtags, username handles, and specific city, state, and country names. However, each token of each tweet used in the model had to be reviewed and manually corrected in order to label uncommon occurrences of entities in the data and to find and correct mistakes made by the dictionary script.

2.3 CRF Classifier

The approach utilized Stanford's Conditional Random Field (CRF) NER system [4]. The CRF NER by accounting for the word before and after the token. This is particularly useful for locations in which there are times, dates, and other indicators of a location. Commonly used words or phrasing, such as, "in", "at", or "here" can be categorized as a location-based reference along with other words. The classifiers observe the sequences and labels and a confidence measure is determined. The feature selection in Figure **1** indicates the features selected for the initial training file.

3 Results

The trained model was tested using a test dataset of hand-tagged, labeled data. The test dataset consisted of approximately 52,000 tokens. The performance of the model was evaluated on the classification according to each entity. Figure 2 shows the precision, recall, and F1 scores for each entity in the dataset. False positives and false negatives were also recorded in the instances where the classification failed to properly identify the entity.
The classification of LOCATION entities did not perform as well as expected due to a number of potential issues. One issue was the sample size of the training set and the number of occurrences of LOCATION entities such as, CITY, STATE, and COUNTRY. Other factors include the limitations of the number of entities used in the CRF classifier. Minimizing the number of entities may improve certain aspects of the model but the granularity of identification for cities, states, and countries may be minimized.

```
#structure of your training file; this tells the classifier
#that the word is in column 0 and the correct answer is in
#column 1
map = word=0,answer=1

#This specifies the order of the CRF: order 1 means that features
#apply at most to a class pair of previous class and current class
#or current class and next class.
maxLeft=1

#these are the features we'd like to train with
#some are discussed below, the rest can be
#understood by looking at NERFeatureFactory
useClassFeature=true
useWord=true
useNGrams=true

#no ngrams will be included that do not contain either the
#beginning or end of the word
noMidNGrams=true
useDisjunctive=true
maxNGramLeng=2
usePrev=true
useNext=true
useSequences=true
usePrevSequences=true
useObservedSequencesOnly=true

#the next 4 deal with word shape features
useTypeSeqs=true
useTypeSeqs2=true
useTypeySequences=true
wordShape=chris2useLC
saveFeatureIndexToDisk = true
qnSize=2

featureDiffThresh=0.05
```

Figure 1. Excerpt from code used in training the NER model.

CRFClassifier tagged 52654 words in 5 documents at 5516.40 words per second.

Entity	P	R	F1	TP	FP	FN
DATE	0.8219	0.5634	0.6685	120	26	93
DIRECTION	0.5275	0.5878	0.5560	144	129	101
EVENT	0.1667	0.0370	0.0606	1	5	26
HASHTAG	0.8703	0.9014	0.8855	1261	188	138
LOC_CITY	0.5839	0.2965	0.3933	94	67	223
LOC_COUNTRY	0.7391	0.5705	0.6439	85	30	64
LOC_MISC	0.0597	0.1290	0.0816	4	63	27
LOC_STATE	0.9091	0.3546	0.5102	50	5	91
LOC_STREET	0.6111	0.1310	0.2157	11	7	73
ORGANIZATION	0.0364	0.0408	0.0385	2	53	47
PERSON	0.4667	0.4639	0.4653	154	176	178
TIME	0.7273	0.6061	0.6612	40	15	26
USERNAME	0.9945	0.9940	0.9942	4309	24	26
Totals	0.8884	0.8371	0.8620	6275	788	1221

Figure 2. Entity classification results.

3.1 Future Work

This work will continue to optimize the model by varying the feature selection within each of the entities identified. Future work will move towards a trained model that can extract geographic named entities within Twitter with better accuracy.

Acknowledgements

The authors acknowledge support through the Space and Naval Warfare Systems Center Atlantic Naval Innovative Science and Engineering (NISE) Program, the Research and Applied Sciences Department, and the Naval Research Enterprise Internship Program.

References

1. Overbey, L. A., Williams, B., Batson, S. C., Williams, L., Greco, B., Bartynski, S., Gonzalez, A. C.: Identifying Firsthand Accounts of Emergencies from Social Media. In: IEEE Technologies for Homeland Security (HST), 2015 IEEE International Symposium, pp. 1–6 (2015)
2. Liu, X., Wei, F., Zhang, S., Zhou, M.: Named entity recognition for tweets.ACM Transactions on Intelligent Systems and Technology (TIST), pp. 3 (2013)
3. Hu, Y., Hong, Y.: Modeling Twitter Engagement in Real-World Events. In: Proceedings of the 50th Hawaii International Conference on System Sciences (2017)
4. Finkel, J.R., Grenager, T., Manning, C.: Incorporating Non-Local Information into Information Extraction Systems by Gibbs Sampling. In: Proceedings of the 43rd Annual Meeting on Association for Computational Linguistics, pp. 363–370 (2005)

A Graph-based Ranking Model for Automatic Keyphrases Extraction from Arabic Documents

Mohamed Salim El Bazzi[1], Driss Mammass[1], Taher Zaki[1], Abdelatif Ennaji[2]

[1]IRF-SIC Laboratory, Faculty of sciences, Ibn Zohr University, Agadir, Morocco
elbazzi.mohamedsalim@edu.uiz.ac.ma; mammass@uiz.ac.ma; t.zaki@uiz.ac.ma
[2]LITIS Laboratory, university of Rouen
Rouen, France, abdel.ennaji@univ-rouen.fr

Abstract: Automatic keyphrases extraction is to extract a set of phrases that are related to the main topics discussed in a document. They have served in several areas of text mining such as information retrieval and classification of a large text collection. Consequently, they have proved their effectiveness. Due to its importance, automatic keyphrases extraction from Arabic documents has received a lot of attention. For instance, the KP-Miner system was proposed to extract Arabic keyphrases, and demonstrates through experimentation and comparison with other systems its effectiveness. In this paper, we introduce TextRank, a graph-based ranking model, used successfully in many tasks of text processing, to compute term weights from graphs of documents. Vertices represent the document's terms, and edges represent term co-occurrence within a fixed window. It is an innovative unsupervised method that we have adapted to extract Arabic keyphrases, and assess its effectiveness. The obtained results with TextRank are compared with those obtained with KPMiner, owing to the fact that both systems do not need a training step.

Keywords: Keyphrases Extraction; KPMiner; TextRank; Arabic Documents.

1 Introduction

Automatic extraction of keyphrases is an important task that allows the synthetic representation and highlighting of important topics in a document. This task facilitates access to relevant documents to ensure better use of the document.

Automatic methods of keyphrases extraction have the particularity to be independent from the domain and the language of the documents to be analyzed. This abstraction is due to the fact that terms are analyzed according to the given document. Many approaches are proposed to this aim, some rely on statistics only, while others combine them with more complex representations of documents.

The task of extracting keyphrases from Arabic documents is becoming increasingly important. In fact, keyphrases can be used to tag digital libraries, to valorize web contents and news streaming, and many more textual data collections. Nevertheless, keyphrases extaction can be a step to improve several text mining applications, including but not limited to classification [1] and information retrieval.

For instance, KP-Miner system [2] is used to extract keyphrases from Arabic documents and demonstrates through experimentation and comparison with widely used systems its effectiveness and efficiency.

Otherwise, Graph ranking algorithms, such as the TextRank [3] have been used successfully in English keyphrases extraction to compute term weights from graphs of a given document, where vertices represent the document's terms, and edges represent term co-occurrence within a fixed window.

Unlike other existing keyphrase extraction systems, the KPMiner and TextRank do not need to be trained in order to achieve their tasks. For this reason, we propose to compare the KPMiner system, considering its outperformance of other keyphrases extraction systems, and TextRank algorithm that we have adapted to extract Arabic keyphrases.

The rest of this paper is organized as following. The second part introduces related works. The third part is dedicated to explain the methods that will be compared in this paper. In the fourth section, we explain the conducted experiments and their results. Finally, we conclude by highlighting some ideas that have been introduced in this work.

2 Related Works

Several approaches attempt to define what a keyphrase is by relying on certain statistical methods and studying the importance of the relationship to the notion of a candidate term. The more important a candidate term is to the analyzed document, the more relevant it is as a keyphrase.

Shishtawy *et al.* in their work [4], add linguistic knowledge to the extraction process, rather than relying only on statistics. They claim that using this approach may provide better results. Their work is based on combining the linguistic knowledge and the machine learning techniques to extract keyphrases from Arabic documents. The proposed system is based on three main steps: Linguistic pre-processing, candidate phrase extraction by generation of N-grams based on their Pos Tags, and feature vector calculation.

Najadat [5] consider the whole phrase which will be nominated as a candidate phrase if its frequency exceeds 2 (exist at least twice within a single paragraph). Phrase frequency (PF), summation of phrase terms frequencies (Tf), PF×IDF (Phrase Frequency–Inverse Document Frequency), Phrase Position, Title Threshold and phrase distribution are the used features in Najadat's approach. The score of each phrase is computed.

Combining linguistic methods with statistical methods could lead to better performance. Thus, Nabil [6] introduces his work using a stemmer and Part of Speech tagger (POS). The stemmer and the POS tagger generate a list of candidate keyphrases. These keyphrases are then weighted by different methods such as TFIDF which still have high performance, according to Nabil, compared to most of the current used methods. The linguistic aspect helps to boost the performance of text mining applications as they add abstract semantic representation to a given document.

Liu *et al.* [7] consider that the best keyphrase must be: understandable, semantically relevant with the document and have high coverage of the whole document. Their method relies on four steps. First, Candidate terms are selected after filtering out the stop words. Second, term relatedness is calculated. They use some measures to calculate the semantic relatedness of candidate terms. The third step is term clustering. Based on term relatedness, they group candidate terms into clusters and find the exemplar terms of each cluster. Finally, they use these exemplar terms to extract keyphrases from the document.

According to EL Baltagy [2], The number and frequency of compound terms in any given document is usually less than that of single keywords. Yet, Effective keyphrase extraction depends on the determination of an appropriate boosting feature for candidate keyphrases. This boosting feature is related to the ratio of single to compound terms in each document. They consider the position of the first occurrence of any given phrase because it is related to the fact that the more important a term is, the more likely it is to appear 'sooner' in the document than later. Nonetheless, they consider also the hypothesis that after a given threshold is passed in any given document, phrases appearing for the first time are highly unlikely to be keyphrases. These observations have been translated into a set of heuristics that are implemented by KPMiner system in three main steps: candidate keyphrase selection, candidate keyphrase weight calculation and final keyphrase refinement.

In the work of Ali *et al* [8]., the authors proceed by document preprocessing including Tokenization, Stop word removal and Stemming. Then, they extract candidate terms by selecting all noun phrases from the Arabic text as candidate Keyphrases. The next step is to extract N- gram phrases from the Arabic phrase. Accordingly, they used POS patterns to identify the candidate noun phrases. Candidate features are extracted by ranking the candidate keyphrase using Term Frequency (TF-IDF). Finally, they introduce a classification process. The idea is to enrich statistical and linguistic information. The keyphrase are used as input to know whether it classifies the term as keyphrase or not. Linear Logistic Regression (LLR), Linear Discriminant Analysis (LDA), Support Vector Machines (SVM) are used for comparison purpose.

The approach of Sarkar [9] is based on four phases. After document preprocessing, candidate keyphrase are identified. A candidate keyphrase is considered as a sequence of words containing no punctuations and stop words, then this sequence is broken into smaller phrases. Afterward, scores are assigned to candidate keyphrases. The weight of a candidate keyphrase is computed using three important features: phrase frequency, inverse document frequency and domain specificity. next, K top-ranked candidate keyphrases are selected as the final list of keyphrases. The value of K is specified by the user.

Mihalcia and tarau present TextRank [3], a Graph-based ranking algorithm to extract keyphrases. The graph based algorithms are a way of deciding the importance of a vertex within a graph. The idea of implementing a graph-based ranking model comes from the concept of recommendation. When one vertex is linked to another one, this connection is considered as a recommendation between those vertices. To fulfill this target, four steps must be accomplished. First of all, to identify text units that best define the document using a Pos tagger and add them as vertices in the graph. Second of all, to identify relations that connect text units, and use these relations to draw edges between vertices in the graph. Edges can be directed or undirected, weighted or unweighted. Third of all, to iterate the graph-based ranking algorithm until convergence. Finally, to sort vertices based on their final score.

Table 1. Overview of related works

Reference	Used methods	Comment
Nabil (2015)	Stemming, Pos Tagging, TFIDF	Combining linguistic methods with statistical methods
Ali(2014)	Preprocessing, TF-IDF	enrich statistical and linguistic information
Mihalcea (2004)	Pos Tagging, TextRank	A Graph based ranking algorithm
El-Beltagy (2009)	KPMiner, frequency	Consider the position of the first occurrence of any given phrase
Elshishtawy (2009)	Linguistic preprocessing, N-grams, Pos Tags, and feature vector calcula-tion.	Combining the linguistic knowledge and the machine learning techni-ques
Najadat (2016)	frequency	Phrase frequency (PF), summation of phrase terms frequencies (Tf), PFIDF (Phrase FrequencyInverse Docu-ment Frequecy), Phrase Position, Title Thre-shold and phrase distribution
Liu (2009)	Preprocessing, term relatedness, clustering.	The best keyphrase must be: understandable, semantically relevant with the document and have high coverage of the whole document
Sarkar (2013)	phrase frequency, inverse document frequency and domain specificity	A candidate keyphrase is considered as a se-quence of words that does not contain neither punctuations nor stop words, and then this sequence is broken into smaller phrases

The extraction of candidate terms is a preliminary step in the extraction of keyphra-ses. If a term of the analyzed document is not present in the set of candidate terms, then the keyphrasee can not be extracted. Used with unsupervised methods, candidate terms are ordered according to an importance score obtained either from themselves or from the importance of the words that compose them. If a method is based only on words, then the score of a candidate term is generally calculated as the sum of the words composing it. However, this is not always fair, so it is an important disadvan-tage of methods working on words to extract key terms. Indeed, the summation may favor words that contain many important words non terms vis-à-vis containing very few words, but important.

3 Arabic Keyphrases Extraction

The unsupervised methods have the particularity to abstract the specific nature of the processed data. This abstraction is due to approaches which valorize semantic importance, degree of informativness, and structure.

3.1 KPMiner

The KPMiner system uses TF-IDF for weighing terms. The use of IDF information for compound phrase weight calculation would improve the extraction of phrases low-frequency phrases. This would build a general rather than a domain-specific exemplar keyphrases extractor, since combinations are much larger.The use of linguistic features will help to extract meaningful keyphrases.

$$TFIDF_{doc}(term) = tf \times idf \quad (1)$$

with

$$idf = \log (N/n_t) \quad (2)$$

tf represents the term frequency, **N** is the total number of documents in the corpus and $\mathbf{n_t}$ the number of documents where the term **t** appears

KPMiner is used to extract Arabic keyphrases and have been compared with KEA extractor [10].

In the experiment, seven, fifteen and twenty keywords were extracted by the system from a document set consisting of 100 Arabic articles. The three systems have been applied to the same dataset to extract extract keyphrases. (Table **2** and **3** show the obtained results).

Table 2. Comparison between developed KP-Miner system and KEA-3.0 [10]

	15 keyphrases		**20 keyphrases**	
	Kpminer	*KEA*	*KPMINER*	*KEA*
Precision	0.143	0.112	0.124	0.092
recall	0.358	0.303	0.376	0.326

3.2. TextRank

TextRank is an adaptation of PageRank for automatic keywords extraction. It is an algorithm proposed by Mihalcea and Tarau [3] that represent text as graph. Each vertex represent a term and point to its predecessors and successors following the reading flow. The score of the vertex v, denoted S (vi), is defined as follows:

Table 3. Comparison between the average F-measure of the developed KP-Miner system and KEA-3.0 when 7, 15, and 20 keyphrases are extracted

	7 keyphrases		**15 keyphrases**		**20 keyphrases**	
	KPMINER	*KEA*	*KPMINER*	*KEA*	*KPMINER*	*KEA*
F-Measure	0.241	0.198	0.205	0.17	0.186	0.143

$$S(v_i) = (1 - d) + d \times \sum_{v_j \in Adj(v_i)} \frac{w_{ji}}{\sum_{v_k \in Adj(v_j)} w_{jk}} S(v_j) \tag{4}$$

Where **Adj (v_j)** represents the neighbors of **v**, and **d** is a damping factor set at 0.85. $\mathbf{w_{ji}}$ is a weight associated to each edge, and represents the frequency of co-occurrence of two words within a window of 2 to10 words. This weight can be any other relationship between words such as, but not limited to, lexical or semantic relations, contextual overlap.

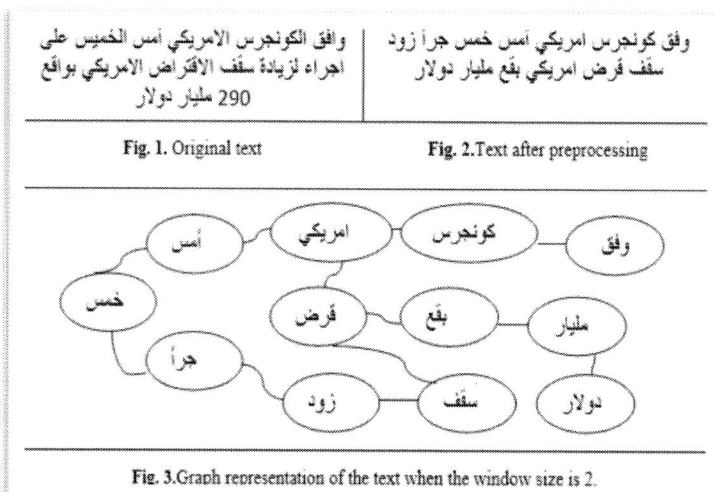

Fig. 1. Original text

Fig. 2.Text after preprocessing

Fig. 3.Graph representation of the text when the window size is 2.

Figure 1. Graph based representation of a document.

For each node of the graph, a score is calculated iteratively to simulate the concept of recommendation of a term by its adjacent nodes. The score at each node grants a ranking value to the word which assesses its importance within the document. Then, the sorted list of words is used to extract keywords.

4 Experiments and Results

The use of a learning corpus implies that the learned models are specific to the subject and the language of it. This specificity can be advantageous when the domain and the language represented by the corpus are the same for the documents which will be analyzed, but if this is not the case, the results of the extraction may decrease.

In this paper, we propose an adaptation of textRank to extract Arabic Keyphrases. For comparison purpose, we introduce in this section two automatic methods. In one hand, we will give an overview of KPMiner which is so far an efficient system of Arabic keyphrases extraction. On the other hand, we will present TextRank algorithm and its adaptation to Arabic language.

4.1. Dataset

To validate the proposed algorithm, we have tested the two systems KPMiner and TextRank on a corpus of 100 documents extracted manually from Al-Jazeera[1]. From each webpage, we extract the "main text" that will represent the processed document, and its related Keys terms "assigned key words" given by Al-Jazeera as illustrated bellow (Figure **2**).

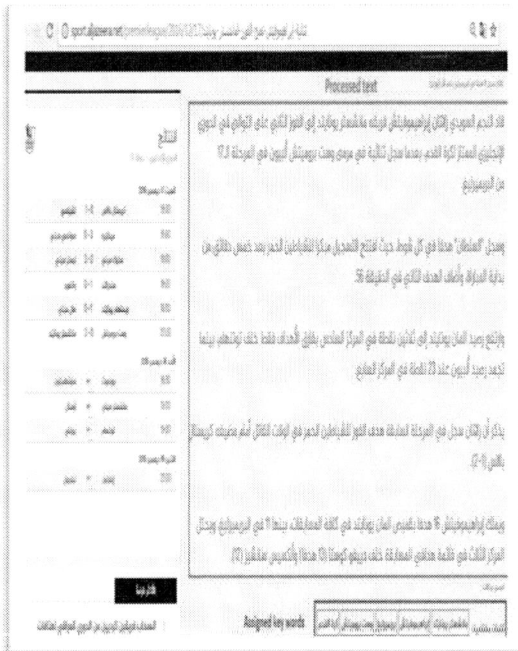

Figure 2. Example of the constructed corpus.

[1]http://www.aljazeera.net

For an efficient validation we have tested the two systems on the same corpus. To evaluate the performance, three conventional metrics are used: precision, recall and F-measure.

4.2. Results

First, we run each system on the main text (documents of corpus) to extract keyphrases. Then, we compare the extracted keyphrases with those assigned by Al-Jazeera to each document. According to KPMiner's results, the most the number of extracted is high, the less it is efficient. So our approach aims to solve this problem. Thus, we select all extracted keyphrases without using any threshold. The following results are drown from the conducted experiments.

Table 4. Comparison between TextRank and KPMiner

	Precision %	**Recall %**	**Fmeasure**
KPminer	7.293	1.162	2.005
TextRank	**14.476**	**4.407**	**6.757**

Table **4** shows that our proposed approach outperforms the KPMiner approach. We can argue this outperformance by two remarks. Firstly, TextRank is a graph-based approach which introduces the concept of recommendation or voting. This concept grant the high score to the each term whitin a structural modeling. In contrast, KPMiner used the bag of word representation which consider that terms are independent in modeling space. Secondly, the used corpus contains a huge variation of topics which complicates the task and influence negatively the efficiency of keyphrases extraction systems when using statistical methods.

5 Conclusion

The keyphrases extraction is a task of analyzing a document and extracting its important aspects. These keyphrases use simple text units to construct a synthetic view of the document. A set of keyphrases can therefore be perceived as one of the text units which key elements are expressed using aggregation between them.

In this paper, we have conducted an experiment to assess the efficiency of adapted TextRank for Arabic document compared with KPminer system. The experimental results show that our proposed method, based on graph modeling of documents, out-performed the KPMiner approach.

In our future work, we will apply Automatic Keyphrases Exctraction from Arabic documents to improve many related fields to Arabic text mining, such as information retrieval. Nonetheless, we will continue to search more suitable approaches to extract Arabic keyphrases.

References

1. Mohamed Salim El Bazzi; Taher Zaki; Driss Mammass; Stemming versus multi-words indexing for Arabic documents classification. 11th International Conference on Intelligent Systems: Theories and Applications (SITA) 2016
2. Samhaa R El-Beltagy and Ahmed Rafea. Kp-miner: A keyphrase extraction system for english and arabic documents. Information Systems, 34(1):132–144, 2009.
3. Mihalcea R. et P. Tarau. Textrank: Bring- ing order into texts. In Proceedings of EMNLP, pages 404–41, 2004.
4. El-shishtawy T.A. & Al-sammak A.K Arabic Keyphrase Extraction using Linguistic knowledge and Machine Learning TechniquesProceedings of the Second International Conference on Arabic Language Resources and Tools, 2009
5. Hassan M. Najadat, Mohammed N. Al-Kabi, Ismail I. Hmeidi, Maysa Mahmoud Bany Issa. Automatic Keyphrase Extractor from Arabic Documents. (IJACSA) International Journal of Advanced Computer Science and Applications, Vol. 7, No. 2, 2016
6. Mahmoud Nabil, Mohamed Aly, Amir F. Atiya. New Approaches for Extracting Arabic Keyphrases. 2015 First International Conference on Arabic Computational Linguistics.
7. Liu, Z. , Peng, L. , Yabin, Z. et S. Maosong. 2009b. Clustering to find exemplar terms for keyphrase extraction. In Proceedings of the 2009 Conference on Empirical Methods in Natural Language Processing, pages 257–266.

8. Nidaa Ghalib Ali, Nazlia Omar. Arabic Keyphrases Extraction Using a Hybrid of Statistical and Machine Learning Methods. International Conference on Information Technology and Multimedia (ICIMU), November 18 – 20, 2014, Putrajaya, Malaysia
9. Kamal Sarkar. A Hybrid Approach to Extract Keyphrases from Medical Documents. International Journal of Computer Applications (0975 – 8887) Volume 63– No.18, February 2013
10. I.H. Witten, *et al.*, KEA: Practical automatic keyphrase extraction, in: The Fourth ACM Conference on Digital Libraries, 1999

Gap in pagination due to unavailable paper.

Pages 85-96

A Graph Data System: Implementation, Algorithms and Applications

Yan Zhang[1], Yiming Wu[2], Tuo Zhu, Yafu Li, Zherui Lu, Qinglong Zhang, Zhi-Jie Zhang, Zheng Xu

[1]Shanghai Chentai Information & Technology CO LTD, Shanghai, China
zhangyan@mana.com
[2]Shanghai Paipaidai Financial Information Service CO LTD, Shanghai, China
wuyiming@ppdai.com

Abstract: For online consumer profiling, a graph based data system has been developed to process hundreds of millions of online events, entities and identities in real-time. The events are online activities like account logins, loan applications and financial transactions; The entities are consumers, mobile devices, banking accounts, etc.; The identifies are the numbers or strings that uniquely identify the entities, *e.g.*, person identification number, mobile phone number, email, etc. Designed on a graph data model, implemented by integrating multiple databases, and deployed on cloud computing platform, the graph based data system is scalable, high performance and fault-tolerance. In the graph data model, the large and complex networks of events and entities, connected by their identities, are treated as a graph of nodes and edges, where nodes represent entities and identities and edges represent connections established by the identities. Based on the model and the graph theory, advanced analytics is applied to develop computational algorithms and software tools, looking for insights and visualizing patterns that are hidden in the data. A MapReduce ranking algorithm is devised and implemented for risk assessment of consumers; An interactive visualization tool is developed for users to explore the inter-relation of the consumers who might be involved in organized frauds. In implementation of the system, a hybrid approach is taken to achieve scalability and high performance, integrating two different types of NoSQL databases into a cohesive data system. The entities and the identities are stored as records and indices, respectively, in key-value tables. Basic database operations, such as load, update and query, are implemented in a Web service with RESTful APIs. The graph based data system is used in an online consumer loan application for profiling loan applicants. The system is invoked directly by a decision making rule engine for verifying the identities and providing credit histories of the applicants.

Keywords. Online Consumer Profiling; Graph Data Model; NoSQL databases; Ranking MR Algorithm; Visualization.

1 Introduction

In online commerce, banking or financing, we often need to process requests for information on events such as:

- account logins
- online loan applications

- online credit card applications
- online transactions

The requests are typically like: verify an account or a customer's identities; review a customer's shopping habits or current interests; and inquire a customer's financial history, *e.g.*, outstanding credits. The information on the consumers is critical for making decisions that have great impact on financial outcomes. As much of the information is collected online, the process is referred to as online consumer profiling in this paper.

In online consumer profiling, customers or devices used to access the internet are referred to as entities:

- persons
- mobile devices
- computers
- accounts

The entities have unique identities which must be verified before any usage to prevent fraud activities, these identities are:

- PID: personal identification number
- mobile: mobile phone number
- home phone number
- home address
- work phone number
- work address
- company name
- email: electronic mail address
- social media accounts: account ids of social media like Facebook and Wechat
- device id: unique identifications of computers or mobile phones; Also known as device fingerprints

A combination of these identities might be needed in identifications of the entities. As events occur in time and geo-locations, in identifications, the events and entities must be considered in the context of time and geo-locations, denoted by time t and geo-locations s, respectively. A consumer online profile consists of events, entities and identities, forming an inter-related network in time and geo-locations as illustrated in Figure **1**.

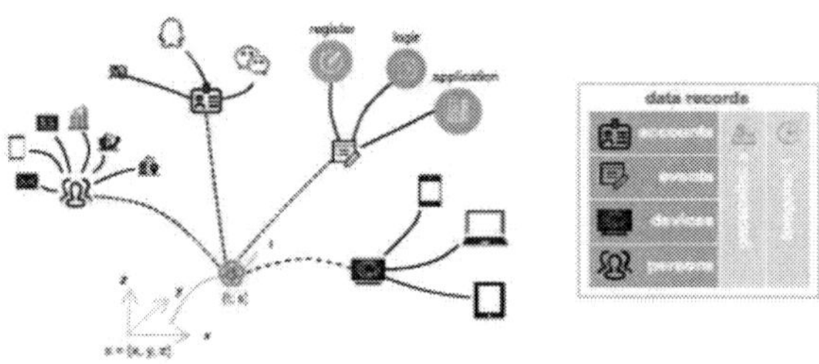

Figure 1. Online consumer profile: events, entities and identities.

In practice, secured, accurate and real-time online consumer profiling is made possible by using some data system that stores a large amount data and makes it readily available for update and query. In this paper, we present a graph based data system for online consumer profiling. Designed for large and complex networks of inter-related profiling data, the data system uses a graph data model to store, update and query records of events and entities.

Use a hybrid approach, the data system is implemented by integrating two NoSQL databases: Cassandra [6] and Elasticsearch [9], in which the entities and the identities are stored as records and indices, respectively, in key-value tables of Cassandra. Elastisearch is used for special search and query of identities or geo-locations:

- identities like names and addresses are not always exact or standard, search and query with fuzzy string matching
- geo-locations are not always precise, search and query in vicinity of a point in latitude and longitude

Basic database operations, loading, updating and querying, are implemented in a Web service with RESTful APIs.

Analytics is an essential part of consumer profiling, providing intelligent insights, quantifying relationship, and visualizing patterns of the data. The graph based data system provides not only the data but also a data model on which the graph theory [14] applies. Based on the model and the theory, a MapReduce [7] ranking algorithm is devised and implemented to score entities based on some known initial values and connectivities. An interactive visualization tool [15] is developed for users to explore the inter-relation of the entities and identities.

In recent years, graph based data stores, visualization tools and algorithms have been developed and applied to various fields [1, 2, 3, 4]. In this paper, the graph based data system is used in an online consumer loan application for profiling loan applicants. The system is invoked directly by a decision making rule engine for verifying the identities and providing credit histories of the applicants.

In the following sections, we present architecture, implementation, analytics, MR algorithm and applications of the graph based data system.

2 Architecture

In design a new data system, we must consider fundamentals of the database: ACID and CAP [5] theorems, and device basic database operations: create, update, delete and query of data records of events, entities and identities. For online consumer profiling, there are some additional requirements:

- Scalability, high performance and fault tolerance: the basic requirements for handling big data
- Low maintenance: easy and low cost to maintain in production
- Analytics: support advanced analytics in providing intelligent insights, quantifying relationship, and visualizing patterns of the data
- Time and geospatial: events occur in time and geo-locations, some data records are considered as temporal and geospatial series

- Fuzzy string matching search and query: names and address are not always precise by ways they are collected, fuzzy string matching search and query need to be supported
- Geospatial search and query: some data records are geospatial series, geospatial search and query need to be supported

It is difficult to meet all these requirements by a single type of common SQL (relational) or NoSQL database, a graph based data system is designed. It is a platform to integrate multiple types of databases into a cohesive data system based on a graph data model.

The graph data model consists a network of nodes and edges representing data records and relationships, respectively. The nodes are the data records of events, entities and identities and edges are the connections established by the identities, see Figure **2**.

The graph data model consists a network of nodes and edges representing data records and relationships, respectively. The nodes are the data records of events, entities and identities and edges are the connections established by the identities, see Figure **2**.

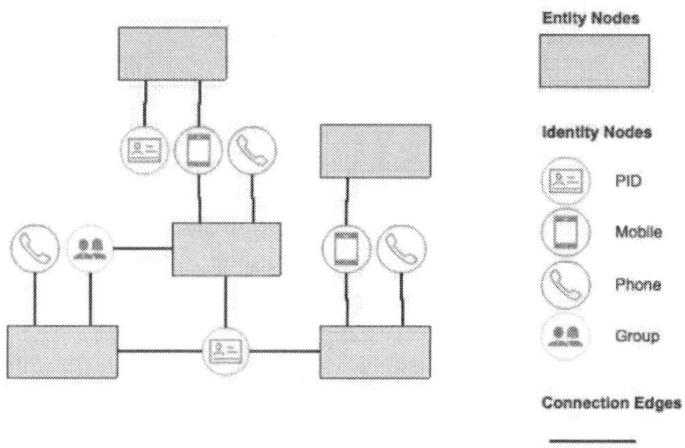

Figure 2. Graph data model.

In the data system, an event is stored as a record which is a list of typed fields:

$$E\ (ID\ ;t,s) = [\ P(ID), O(ID), D(ID)\ ; t,s] \qquad (1)$$

where ID is a list of identities, t is date time and s is location, t and s are context parameters indicating when and where the event occurs; P(ID), O(ID) and D(ID) are the lists of the entities; P(ID) is the person list:

$$P(ID)\ = [\ ID;\ p\ ] \qquad (2)$$

where p is a list of person properties, *e.g.*, name, age and favorite merchant items; O(ID) is the object list, *e.g.*, a car with properties like make, type and year; And D(ID) is the device list, *e.g.*, a mobile phone with properties of phone number and

MAC address. Entities P(ID), O(ID) and D(ID) are related by ID and context parameters t and s through events E(ID; t, s). Entities are stored as records in the record tables with format:

$$rec = [\,RID, value;\ t, s] \tag{3}$$

where RID is the record id or key; value is a JSON document with properties of the entities. As noticed, it is a key-value type data table. Each identities are stored as indices or references in the reference tables with format:

$$ref = [\,ID, types, RID\,] \tag{4}$$

where ID is the identity; types are identity type and record types which can be used as filtering parameters; and RID is the record id in (3). The data system and relation between reference and record is shown in Figure **3**.

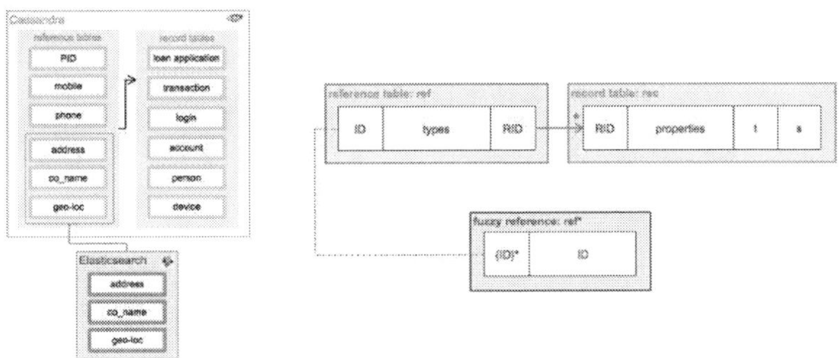

Figure 3. Hybrid data system.

3 Implementation

The graph based data system has been developed, using the graph data model and a hybrid approach, multiple databases, Cassandra and Elasticsearch, are integrated into a cohesive data system (see Fig 3). Cassandra is a scalable, high performance, distributed and NoSQL database, designed to handle large amounts data across many commodity servers. Cassandra data table is of key-value type. For record tables, keys are RIDs and values are JSON documents containing the properties of entities. For reference tables, keys are identities, values are RIDs of the records. For indices like names and addresses, identities are also loaded in Elasticsearch search engine for queries that require fuzzy string matching. Elasticsearch is a distributed and scalable search engine based on Lucene. Elasticsearch is also used to store geo-locations for geospatial queries.

Database basic operations of load and query are implemented by invoking APIs of Cassandra and Elasticsearch.

To load a record, the following steps are taken:

1. Create a UUID as RID of the record

2. Form a JSON document using properties of the record
3. Insert RID and JSON document into a record table
4. Extract IDs from the record
5. Insert IDs and corresponding RIDs into reference tables
6. If fuzzy string matching queries are needed, take additional additional steps:

(a) Standardize the strings

(b) `Load the strings into Elasticsearch tables

The whole load process is shown in Figure **4**.

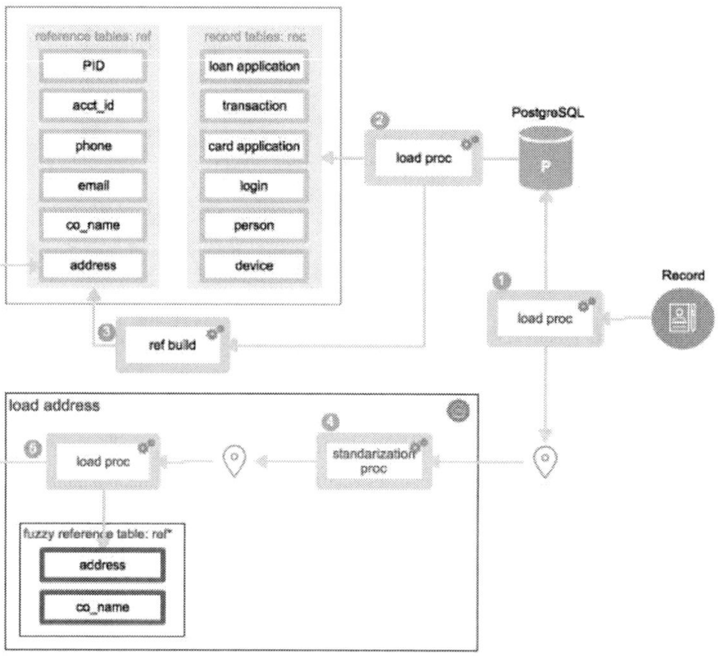

Figure 4. Load process.

Query or traversal operations are implemented for two basic types of queries: breadth-first and depth-first search, configurations are possible for these parameters:

- Connection set: entities are connected by a specific set of identities
- Time window: records of entities with timestamp, traversal operation return entities within the specified time window.
- Graph depth: breath-first or depth-first search terminates once the specified depth is reached

We deployed the system on a cloud system, the entire data system includes an Elasticsearch cluster, a Cassandra cluster and an API server cluster to provide unified

RESTful API to access backend databases. The Elasticsearch includes 3 nodes and the Cassandra cluster includes 6 nodes. Each of the storage nodes has 4 cores, 16GB memory and 1 TB SSD mounted on the cloud system with 10G bandwidth internal network. The API server cluster includes 2 nodes, each has 4 cores and 8GB memory.

4 Analytics

The graph based data system stores consumer profiling data in a graph data structure with massive amount information. Analytics is called for to develop computational algorithms and software tools for information discovery, looking for financial insights, quantifying relationships for automated decision-makings, and visualizing hidden patterns.

For online consumer profiling, consumer ranking on certain subject is often conducted to find a consumer's relative position in a group, each consumer is assigned to a score based on known scores of a small sample and connectivities of the group. For example, a group of consumers are connected by identities of PID and mobile, and a number of members are found to be involved in some fraud activities, which pose great risk for online financial companies. Assign highest scores as initial values for these consumers, scores of the rest are calculated based on the initial values and group connectivities. Here the scores represent consumer risks in future online activities.

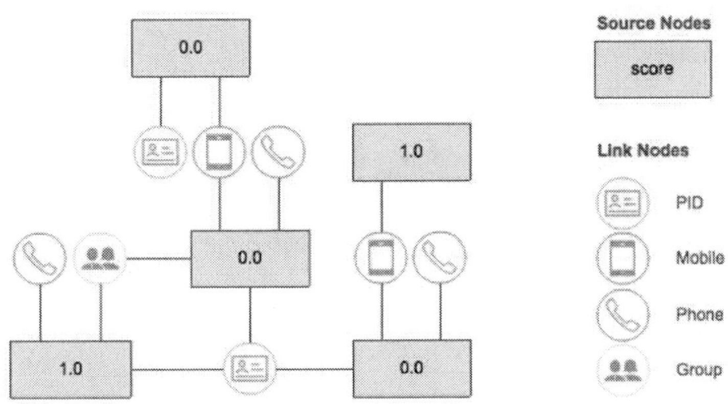

Figure 5. Graph with initial scores.

A consumer ranking algorithm is devised and implemented, in which scores are calculated iteratively based on initial scores and a graph model of nodes and edges as illustrated in Figure **5**. The algorithm converges to the solution which is the desired score distribution as demonstrated by an example. The mathematical proof of convergence is provided.

The profiling data is retrieved from the graph based data system, the connectivity is well defined in the graph data structure. As the data size is large, computation will be most effectively carried out on a cluster of computers in parallel, the algorithm employs a MapReduce design pattern will be presented in next section.

From analysis perspectives, as illustrated in Figure **5**, there are two types of nodes in the graph: source nodes and link nodes. Source and link nodes are the property nodes for the entities and identities, respectively.

Let $\mathbf{s} = \{s_i\}$ denote scores of source nodes and $r = \{r_i\}$ denote scores of link nodes with

$$s_i \; for \; i = 1,2,\cdots,N \tag{5}$$

N is the number of source nodes, and

$$r_i \; for \; i = 1,2,\cdots,M \tag{6}$$

M is the number of link nodes.

Given initial scores of source nodes:

$$s_i^0 \; for \; i = 1,2,\cdots,N \tag{7}$$

an iterative procedure is constructed to obtain scores distribution for all nodes including those of link nodes. In a recurrence formula for $n = 1,2,\ldots$, the nth iteration is given below:

1. Let S_i be a set of source nodes directly connected to the ith link node, the score r_i of ith link node is calculated by averaging scores of source nodes which are directly connected to ith link node:

$$r_i^{(n)} = \frac{1}{|S_i|}\sum_{j\in S_i} s_j^{(n-1)} \; for \; i = 1,2,\cdots,M \tag{8}$$

where $|S_i|$ is the size of S_i.

2. Let R_i be a set of link nodes directly connected to the ith source node, the score r_i of ith source node is calculated by averaging scores of link nodes which are directly connected to ith source node:

$$s_i^{(n)} = (1-\beta)s_i^{(0)} + \beta\bar{s}_i^{(n)} \; for \; i = 1,2,\cdots,N \tag{9}$$

where $0 < \beta < 1$ is a parameter introduced to add weighted initial scores $s_i^{(0)}$ to the results; and

$$\bar{s}_i^{(n)} = \frac{1}{|R_i|}\sum_{j\in R_i} r_j^{(n)} \tag{10}$$

where $|R_i|$ is the size of R_i.

3. Let ε be a small number of relative error, if

$$\max_{i=1}^{N}\frac{|s_i^{(n+1)} - s_i^{(n)}|}{|s_i^{(n)}|} < \varepsilon \tag{11}$$

let $s_i^* = s_i^{(n+1)}$ and exit the procedure; Otherwise, return to step 1 and continue the iteration.

The solution s_i^* for $i = 1,2,\ldots,N$ are obtained.

In each iteration, scores of link and source nodes are calculated in separate steps, namely, (8) and (9). Each link node score is calculated by averaging scores of surrounding source nodes; Likewise, each source node score is calculated by averaging scores of surrounding link nodes. The algorithm is well suited for implementation in MapReduce design pattern. As shown below, in the matrix form, a positive-definite operator is constructed, the iterations converge.

To provide proof of convergence, the adjacency matrix $\mathbf{A} = [a_{ij}]$ is introduced, where

$$a_{ij} = \begin{cases} 1 & if\ nodes\ i\ and\ j\ are\ directly\ connected\ ; \\ 0 & otherwise\ . \end{cases} \tag{12}$$

it defines the connectivities of the graph. In adjacency matrix, (8) and (10) are written as:

$$\mathbf{r}^{(n)} = \mathbf{SAs}^{(n-1)} \tag{13}$$

where $\mathbf{S} = diag(\frac{1}{|S_1|}, \frac{1}{|S_2|}, \cdots, \frac{1}{|S_M|})$ is a diagonal matrix, and

$$\bar{\mathbf{s}}^{(n)} = \mathbf{A}^T\mathbf{Rr}^{(n)} \tag{14}$$

where $\mathbf{R} = diag(\frac{1}{|R_1|}, \frac{1}{|R_2|}, \cdots, \frac{1}{|R_N|})$ is a diagonal matrix. Matrices $\mathbf{SA}$ and $\mathbf{A}^T\mathbf{R}$ are scaled adjacency matrix. Without lose of generality, replace $|S_i|$ and $|R_i|$ in (8) and (10) by a parameter d:

$$d = \max_{m,n}(|S_m|, |R_n|) \tag{15}$$

It is noted that d is the maximum number of connected nodes for a source or link node in the graph. Equations (13) and (14) are written as:

$$\mathbf{r}^{(n)} = \bar{\mathbf{A}}\mathbf{s}^{(n-1)} \tag{16}$$

and

$$\bar{\mathbf{s}}^{(n)} = \bar{\mathbf{A}}^T\mathbf{r}^{(n)} \tag{17}$$

where the scaled adjacency matrix $\bar{\mathbf{A}} = [\bar{a}_{ij}]$ is defined as:

$$\bar{a}_{ij} = \begin{cases} 1/d & if\ nodes\ i\ and\ j\ are\ directly\ connected\ ; \\ 0 & otherwise\ . \end{cases} \tag{18}$$

It should be noted that:

$$\| \bar{\mathbf{A}} \|_1 \leq 1 \tag{19}$$

where $\|\cdot\|_1$ is 1-norm of a matrix.

From (9), in matrix form,

$$\mathbf{s}^{(n)} = (1-\beta)\mathbf{s}^{(0)} + \beta\bar{\mathbf{s}}^{(n)} \tag{20}$$

Combine (20), (17) and (16), we have

$$\mathbf{s}^{(n)} = (1-\beta)\mathbf{s}^{(0)} + \mathbf{Bs}^{(n-1)} \tag{21}$$

where

$$\mathbf{B} = \beta\bar{\mathbf{A}}^T\bar{\mathbf{A}} \tag{22}$$

and $\mathbf{B}$ is symmetric and positive definite with properties:

$$\rho(\mathbf{B}) \leq \| \mathbf{B} \|_1 \leq \beta \| \bar{\mathbf{A}}^T \|_1 \| \bar{\mathbf{A}} \|_1 < 1 \tag{23}$$

where $\rho(\mathbf{B})$ is the spectral radius of **B** [13].

In recurrence, (21) can be written explicitly in $\mathbf{s}^{(0)}$ for $n > 0$:

$$\mathbf{s}^{(n)} = \mathbf{B}^n \mathbf{s}^{(0)} + (1-\beta)[\textstyle\sum_{i=0}^{n-1} \mathbf{B}^i]\mathbf{s}^{(0)} \tag{24}$$

As $n \to \infty$, from the above equation:

$$\lim_{n\to\infty} \mathbf{s}^{(n)} = \lim_{n\to\infty} \mathbf{B}^n \mathbf{s}^{(0)} + (1-\beta)\lim_{n\to\infty}[\textstyle\sum_{i=0}^{n-1} \mathbf{B}^i]\mathbf{s}^{(0)} \tag{25}$$

Since $\rho(\mathbf{B}) < 1$ as shown in (23), we have:

$$\lim_{n\to\infty} \mathbf{B}^n \mathbf{s}^{(0)} = 0 \tag{26}$$

and

$$\lim_{n\to\infty} \textstyle\sum_{i=0}^{n-1} \mathbf{B}^i = (\mathbf{I} - \mathbf{B})^{-1} \tag{27}$$

(25) becomes:

$$\lim_{n\to\infty} \mathbf{s}^{(n)} = (1-\beta)(\mathbf{I} - \mathbf{B})^{-1}\mathbf{s}^{(0)} \tag{28}$$

The iterations (21) converge [13].

To demonstrate, an example of consumer fraud risk ranking is shown here. We have a group of consumers who are connected by their PIDs and mobile numbers as shown in Fig 6, where the initial scores are given based on known fraud risks of some consumers. For those we don't have any fraud information except their connections, the initial scores are set to be 0.

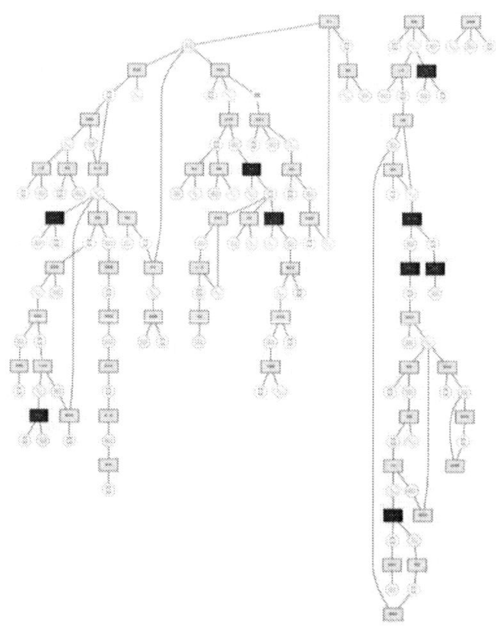

Figure 6. Example: Graph and initial scores.

Using the algorithm, set $\beta = 0.95$ and and $\varepsilon = 0.01$, we obtain the solutions in 12 iterations, the results are shown in Fig 7. The color grad represents the level of risk.

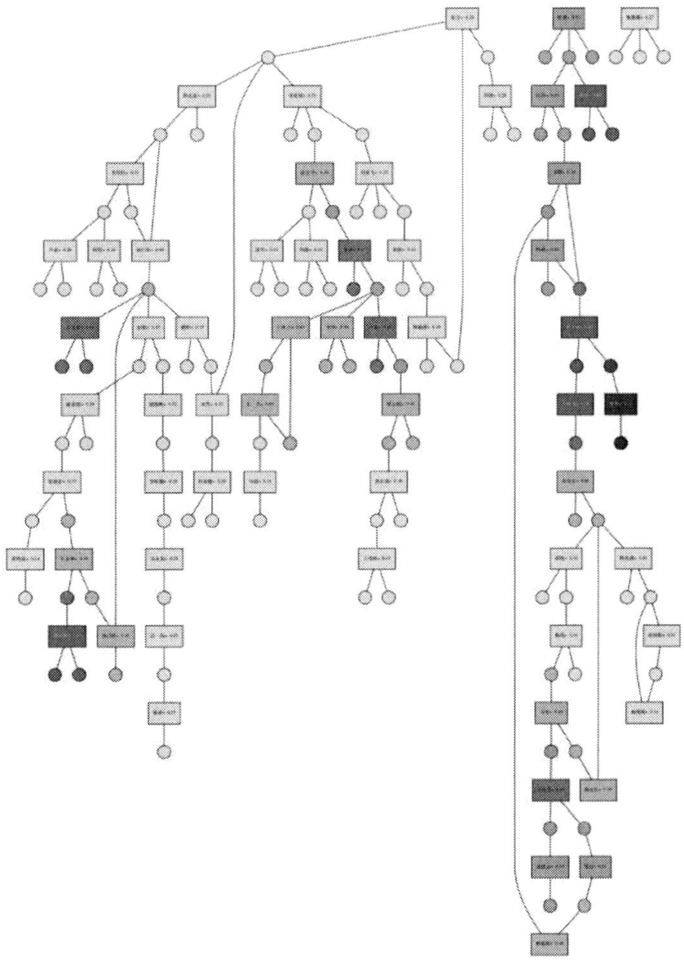

Figure 7. Example: Final scores.

5 MapReduce Algorithm

For consumer ranking graph with millions of source and link nodes, computation must be carried out on a cluster of computers (nodes) in parallel. For the computation procedure described in previous section, an algorithm is developed on MapReduce framework.

MapReduce is a programming model for processing large-scale data [7], in which data processing is divided into two phases: map and reduce. The map phase is responsible for processing given (key, value) pairs stored on the distributed file system and generating intermediate (key, value) pairs. In the reduce phase, intermediate pairs with the same key are collected, processed at once, and stored as the results to the distributed file system.

In MapReduce model, communication between different computer nodes only takes place during a single communication phase, when the intermediate pairs from the map nodes are transferred to the reduce nodes. Apart from this, no further communication takes place. Neither do the individual mappers nor the individual reducers communicate with each other. This loose coupling of the computational nodes enables the framework to perform the calculations in a highly distributed and fault-tolerant way. Since all computational nodes process the data independently from each other, the only limitation for the number of parallel reducer-jobs is the number of unique intermediate key values. Additionally, since the single jobs do not depend on the results of other jobs, the failure of hardware can be easily managed by restarting the same job on another computational node. This high fault-tolerance and the loose coupling of computational nodes suits perfectly for usage of this model on commodity hardware like personal PCs connected to a cluster over a network. However, this limited communication also poses a challenge for the development of algorithms, which have to be designed such that the data in different mappers/reducers can be processed completely independently. Especially, the results computed by different reducers can not be combined in a MapReduce job. Thus, many problems cannot be solved using a single MapReduce job, but have to be solved by a chain of MapReduce jobs, such that the result records of one iteration can be re-distributed to the reducers and thus combined in the next iteration.

For ranking consumers in the graph, the idea is to iteratively alter growing local parts of the graph until scores of all source and link nodes converge. In initialization, a data structure is prepared as:

$$[\, source\ node\, ,\, link\ node\, ,\, initial\ score\,] \tag{29}$$

where the source node has three members: id, current score and last score. Iterations follow the steps described in Section 4. The algorithm is listed in Algorithm 1.

The algorithm has been programed using Apache Spark framework. In general, there are five MapReduce jobs to be executed in the each iteration. And each MapReduce job can be simply implemented by Apache Spark framework. Apache Spark offers in-memory capabilities so each MapReduce jobs can be completed in short time and the whole job can converge fast if the number of iterations is small. Remarkably, we only need to persist the last RDD in memory using cache() method at the end of each iteration.

6 APPLICATIONS

The graph based data system has been employed in a software system processing online loan applications, where each applicants' identities and credit histories are verified and reviewed to determine credit default risks. The system is required to provide these information in real-time:

Algorithm 1 Traversal Ranking Iteration Handler (MR Version)

procedure ITERHANDLER($iteration_{max}$, $tolerance_{max}$, $data$, $beta$)
    $iteration_{current} = 0$
    $tolerance_{current} = 0$
    while $iteration_{current} \leq iteration_{max}$ **do**
        R-Phase: $r_{list} \leftarrow [(s,\ r,\ score_s^r),\ \ldots]$
        M-Phase: $r_{score} \leftarrow [(r,\ [s_1^r,\ s_2^r,\ \ldots],\ sum(score_s^r),\ \ldots]$
        R-Phase: $r_{score}^{total} = sum([item[-1],\ \ldots])\ for\ item\ \in\ r_{score}$
        M-Phase: $r_{score}^{norm} \leftarrow [(item[0],\ item[1],\ item[-1]\ /\ r_{score}^{total}),\ \ldots]\ for\ item\ \in\ r_{score}$
        MR-Phase: $s_{list} \leftarrow\ Group\ [(s,\ item[0],\ item[-1]),\ \ldots]\ for\ s\ \in\ item[1]\ ,for\ item\ \in\ r_{score}^{norm}\ By\ s$
        M-Phase:
        for each s_i in s_{list} **do**
            $s_i^r = [for\ r\ \in\ s_i]$
            $s_i^{score} = (1-beta) * s_i.init_{score} + beta * sum([r.score^{norm}\ \ldots]\ for\ r\ \in s_i^r)$
        end for
        MR-Phase: $tolerance = sum([(s^{score}\ -\ s_{last}^{score})^2,\ \ldots]\ for\ s\ \in\ s_{list})$
        if $tolerance < tolerance_{max}$ **then**
            break
        end if
        M-Phase: $data \leftarrow [(s,\ r,\ s^{score}\ /\ length\ of\ [r,\ \ldots])]\ for\ r\ \in\ s\ ,for\ s\ \in\ s_{list}$
    end while
    Return s_{list}
end procedure

- if the applicant has applied the credit at same or other organizations in passed 18 months.
- if the contact persons provided by the applicant have applied the credits in passed 18 months.
- if the applicant is related to persons on the high risk list by any means like mobile number, PID or address.
- if the applicant is associated with any known fraud organizations as a participant or victim.

The workflow is shown in Fig 8, where two modules depend on the graph based data system directly: rule engine and case manager.

In rule engine, applicant's information is retrieved in scripts using a set of RESTful APIs. In case manager, which is a Web application, applicant's information is explored interactively.

- *ad hoc* search and query: enter pid, mobile number or addresses to check if the applicant is on high risk list
- visualize relevant information: point-and-click on the items to get detailed information and to view relations to other persons as shown in Fig 9. To gain detailed information, tools like zooming and filtering are provided.

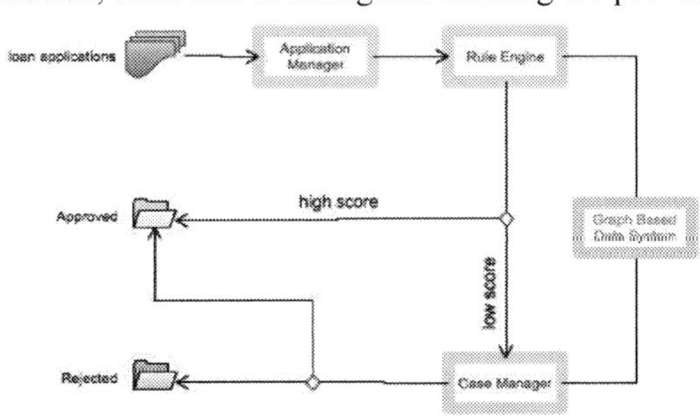

Figure 8. Online loan application system.

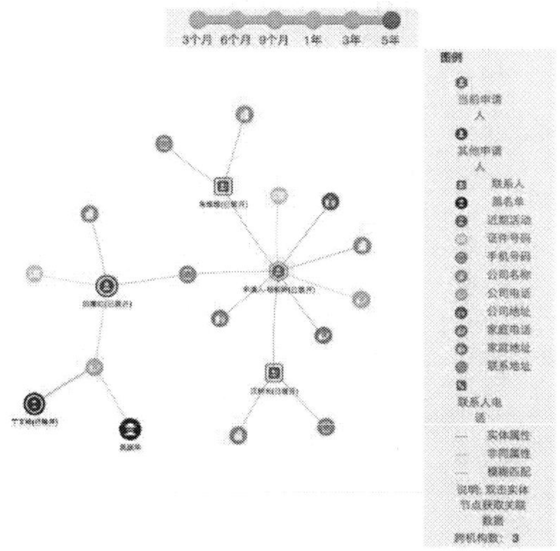

Figure 9. Visualization tool.

References

1. neo4j, https://neo4j.com/
2. P. Perner and W. Paetzold, An Incremental Learning System for Image Interpretation, Shape, Structure and Pattern Recognition, P. Perner, W. Pätzold, D. Dori and A. Bruckstein (Eds.), World Scientific Publishing Co, pages 311–323 (1995)
3. P. Perner, Case-base maintenance by conceptual clustering of graphs, Engineering Applications of Artificial Intelligence, 19(4), pages 381–295 (2006)
4. V.P.Eswaramoorthy, New algorithm for analyzing performance of neighborhood strategies in solving job shop scheduling problems, Journal of Scientific & Industrial Research, 67(08), pages 579–588 (2008)
5. Eric Brewer: CAP twelve years later: How the "rules" have changed, Computer, 45(2), pages 23–29 (2012)
6. Apache Cassandra. http://cassandra.apache.org/
7. J. Dean and S. Ghemawat, MapReduce: Simplified Data Processing on Large Clusters. Sixth Symposium on Operating System Design and Implementation (OSDI04), San Francisco, CA (2004)
8. Emden R. Gansner and Stephen C. North, An open graph visualization system and its applications to software engineering, AT&T Labs - Research, Shannon Laboratory, 180 Park Avenue, Florham Park, NJ 07932, USA (1999)
9. Elasticsearch. https://www.elastic.co/
10. T. Haerder and A. Reuter, Principles of transaction-oriented database recovery. ACM Computing Surveys. 15 (4): 287. doi:10.1145/289.291 (1983)
11. L. Page, S. Brin, R. Motwani, and T. Winograd, The pagerank citation ranking: Bringing order to the web. Technical Report 1999-66, Stanford InfoLab, November 1999. Previous number = SIDL-WP-1999-0120 (1999)
12. Spark Overview, http://spark.apache.org/docs/latest/
13. David M. Young, Iterative Solution of Large Linear Systems, Academic Press (1971)
14. Robin J. Wilson, Introduction to Graph Theory, 4th edition, Prentice Hall (1996)
15. Emden R. Gansner and Stephen C. North, An open graph visualization system and its applications to software engineering, AT&T Labs - Research, Shannon Laboratory, 180 Park Avenue, Florham Park, NJ 07932, USA (1999).

Performance Analysis of Sparks Machine Learning Library

S. Yasrobi, J. Alston, B. Yadranjiaghdam and N. Tabrizi

East Carolina University, Department of Computer Science, Science and Technology Building, Greenville, NC 27858-4353 USA
Phone: +1-252-412-1179
yasrobis14@students.ecu.edu; alstonja14@students.ecu.edu; yadranjiaghdamb15@studentds.ecu.edu; tabrizim@ecu.edu

Abstract: This paper examines the performance of Apache Sparks machine learning library with reference to the optimal required resources such as number of machines and cores to best perform popular machine learning algorithms. In order to achieve this, we have observed training time of classification algorithms such as logistic regression, support vector machines, decision trees, random forests, and gradient boosted trees under different configurations on a sample dataset. Our research revealed that having excessive number of resources does not necessarily decrease the training time of the machine learning algorithms, it may even degrade the training time by up to 30 percent. Furthermore, this study confirms that methodologies such as tree ensembles can increase the training time of machine learning algorithms compared to that of typical decision trees.

1 Introduction

Machine learning with its automated learning power unleashes big datas power to aid data scientists to gain knowledge in variety of applications such as computer vision, speech processing, natural language understanding, neuroscience, health, and Internet of Things (IoT). The major challenges of using machine learning in big data is to perform the analysis in a reasonable time [28].

In-memory processing with its increased performance in response time has been proven beneficial in a range of areas such as fraud detection, risk management, and decision-making, where machine learning algorithms are used to conduct analytics. Together with real-time analytics it provides unmatched productivity and profit gains that explains why companies such as Facebook, Twitter, and Amazon take advantage of their capabilities [9,24].

In-memory processing involves querying data in computerâ€™s RAM instead of its hard disk. Being able to interact directly with RAM as opposed to the traditional method of hard disks I/O operations greatly increases response times and throughput. Acker *et al.* concluded that response times were 5 to 19 times better and throughput increased by 7 times when using in-memory processing platforms. It has been reported that in-memory processing is easier to set up and maintain which is ideal when analyzing large datasets [1], reduction in memory prices, and higher user satisfaction that enables faster data access that contributes to faster decision making. [5, 10, 12].

There are various big data frameworks that take advantage of in-memory processing and of those frameworks the one that is mostly used is Apache Spark, a descendent of Hadoop. Using its in-memory capabilities Apache Spark executes machine learning algorithms efficiently by keeping the dataset in RAM and eliminating the repetitious pulling of data from the hard disk [14]. For example, the machine learning algorithm known as logistic regression is over 100 times faster when using Spark instead of Hadoop [3].

Spark has caused a surge of interest due to companies desire to utilize real-time analytics, analysis of streaming IoT data sets, and efficient implementation of iterative algorithms. But regardless of its benefits, unfamiliarity of many companies with big data cluster specifications such as the number of machines, number of cores per machine, and the interoperability of machines, often results in lower hardware usage efficiency. Every data analysis ecosystem has two main components which are filesystem and processing system. Spark, handles files in the form of Resilient Distributed Datasets (RDD), and processes them with its in-memory processing engine. In the following sections, we discuss more about these components as well as our choice of test data set and algorithms.

1.1 Resilient Distributed Dataset

RDDs are data structures that partition the dataset into multiple partitions, and aid with parallel computing by supporting iterative operations on the Spark. The resilient feature of RDD that logs the transformations used to build a dataset will capture enough information to re-compute a lost or damaged partition. Furthermore, RDD gives users control over how the data is partitioned, the storage strategy for each RDD, and indicate which RDDs will be reused. Due to its parallel computing capabilities, RDD significantly improves the performance of large dataset computations on an in-memory computing platform [26].

1.2 In-memory Processing

In-memory processing has been studied since the 1980â€™s, but recently it has gained popularity due to the availability of ultra-fast memories, each with its massive capacity often offered at the lower cost [23, 13]. There are several significant differences between processing in main memory versus processing on hard disks. The most quantifiable difference is the fact that main memory processes computations notably faster than hard disks [11]. This is because in-memory processing places the computation near the data as means to reduce data movement [2]. Despite the volatility and vulnerability of main memory, the processing speed and other benefits makes using in-memory processing worthwhile.

1.3. Data

In this study, Higgs dataset from UCI machine learning repository [4] has been adopted and produced using Monte Carlo simulations. The first 21 features are kinematic properties measured by the particle detectors in the accelerator and the last seven features are functions of the first 21 features; these are high-level features derived by to help discriminate between the two classes.

1.4. Machine Learning Algorithms

Machine learning is a type of artificial intelligence that provides computers with the ability to learn autonomously, using a combination of methodologies developed by the statisticians and computer scientists, to learn relationships from data while also placing emphasis on efficient computing algorithms. Machine learning is also used in the analysis and diagnosis for medical images in radiological medicine, predict the susceptibility of soil liquefaction, and forecast models of consumer credit risk. The techniques used within these countless applications of machine learning techniques each fall under one of two categories of supervised or unsupervised learning [8, 25, 20, 15].

In this study, we have examined the performance of the following five machine learning algorithms.

1) Logistic Regression: Linear regression attempts to fit a line to data that has only two levels or outcomes, whereas, logistic regression models the chance of an outcome based on a transformation known as a logit [19]. Spark uses two optimizers that are examined for logistic regression in this study. These optimizers are Stochastic Gradient Descent (SGD) and Limited Memory BFGS (LBFGS).

The SGD approximates the gradient by accessing a single element within the dataset during each iteration. It works best for machine learning algorithms that are large in magnitude because it does not require loading the entire dataset. It is also inexpensive in regards to computations and the dataset can be quickly processed. Those benefits are key factors that influence many to use SGD to optimize logistic regression and SVM algorithms [22]. LBFGS is a quasi-Newton method optimizer that uses prior iterations to estimate the Hessian matrix of the objective function [27]. These prior iterations have a sequence of gradient vectors that are used to solve unconstrained nonlinear minimization problems. Of the machine algorithms that were previously mentioned, logistic regression utilizes LBFGS to optimize its performance.

2) Support Vector Machine (SVM): The support vector machine algorithm uses training examples to create a hyperplane that separates the dataset into classes. The complexity of classes may vary, but the simplest form of the SVM algorithm has only two possible labels to choose from. To reduce misclassifications, a decision boundary is obtained while training the SVM algorithm. This decision boundary is known as the optimal separation hyperplane [22]. The only optimizer available for SVM on Spark is SGD optimizer.

3) Decision Trees: Classification *via* decision trees begins with a series of questions about the various features of the dataset. Each question is housed in a node that points to at least one child node that responds to the question. A hierarchal tree is formed as a result of these questions and thus, allowing the classification of an item based on how we answer the questions. A classification occurs once we have reached a leaf node [16].

4) Random Forests: Random forests and boosted trees are other forms of classifiers that are based on decision trees and yield more precise classifications by its multiple decision trees. Random forests are one of the methods of tree ensembles where tree predictors are combined in such a way that each trees prediction depends on the values of a random vector sampled independently and with the same distribution for all trees in the forest. In process of training a random forests predictor model, the root node corresponds to whole input space and this input space will be partitioned into multiple disjoint partitions. At each of these nodes, a decision tree model will be trained based on its data partition [6].

5) Gradient Boosted Trees: One of the common methods for improving accuracy of any machine learning algorithm is by boosting it. This method has been introduced by Sapphire at 1990 and utilizes a combination of weak classifiers in order to create a sturdier classification model. Gradient boosted trees classification algorithm allows for first decision tree model to be trained based on the training dataset, improving the accuracy of the model iteratively by retraining the model. During each training, tuples will be reweighted, so the model can decrease its error rate. Boosting does not suffer from overfitting regularly, but because of its iterative nature takes longer time to train the model [7].

2 Related Works

Until recently, there has not been much research conducted in regards to in-memory processing. Sparkâ€™s in-memory capabilities have been shown to be faster and more flexible than Hadoop in a variety of areas [21]. For example, according to study reported in [26], a workload that took 20 hours on Hadoop was reduced to 3 minutes on Spark. The performance of in-memory processing is analyzed with regard to the number of machines, amount of memory, number of cores per machine, and the amount of pool threads on a variety of workloads [2]. Machine learning is treated as a small aspect instead of a focal point.

Siegal *et al.* [21] presented a machine-learning library prototype called Smart-MLib that allows machine learning implementations to be invoked from a program other than Spark. The authors tested the library's performance, and built machine-learning applications that are also provided in Spark's MLlib and tested the performance of k-means clustering, linear regression, Gaussian mixture models, and support vector machines using MLib and Smart-Mlib.

Kumar *et al.* [17] compared the prediction accuracy of two groups of supervised machine learning ensembles based Meta learners. They showed that Random Forest performs well in both Meta learners: bagging and boosting than other learning algorithms. Lee *et al.* [18] evaluated the performance of three sampling-based algorithms, four ensemble algorithms, four instance-based algorithms, and two support vector machine algorithms. They conducted two experiments to compare algorithm performance using etching process data and chemical vapor deposition process data, which showed that increasing imbalance ratio leads to higher performance in the instance-based algorithms.

3 Big Data Infrastructure

3.1. Hardware

Big Data analytics require a scalable hardware infrastructure with parallel processing capability. This system should have enough memory, bandwidth, and throughput to run multiple tasks simultaneously, and perform parallel processing of advanced analytics algorithms in matter of seconds. Since the main concept of Big Data computing is distributed processing, in this study the framework is implemented over a cluster of servers. We have arranged a cluster of 16 servers providing a powerful hardware base for big data analytics tasks. Four of these servers act as administrative nodes, and 12 servers operate as worker nodes. Each of the 16 servers have two Intel(R) Xeon(R) quad core CPU 5620 2.40 GHz processors, meaning there are eight real cores or 16 virtual cores on each server. The servers are equipped with 16 GB DDR3 RAM and a 1 TB hard disk. The operating system used is a Linux Ubuntu server 14.04 64-bit distribution. The switch used is Juniper EX4200, which is a high-performance, low-latency, and provides a one Gigabit Ethernet (GbE) access environment.

3.2. Software

To analyze the performance of machine learning algorithms on Spark, we began by building a Hadoop cluster using YARN as the resource manager. YARN is a platform that provides consistent operations, security, and data governance tools across Hadoop clusters. We chose YARN as the resource manager because it outperforms Sparks standalone mode for handling clusters. YARN allows for multi-tenancy, dynamic allocation of cluster resources, and data center expansion [Siegal et~al(2016)Siegal, Guo, and Agrawal]. A bash script was created that ran machine learning models on the HIGGS dataset with data size of 8 gigabytes, 28 attributes, and 11 million instances [Baldi etal. (2014)Baldi, Sadowski, and Whiteson]. To test the performance of the machine learning algorithms, we utilized a maximum of 7 machines with 8 virtual cores and 16 gigabytes of RAM. The amount of data partitions were also taken into account when analyzing the performance of the machine learning algorithms. There were a range of 40 to 60 partitions used. The performance time of the machine learning algorithms were first averaged in regards to the number of machines and then averaged by the number of cores. 1) Spark: Spark is a framework for parallel processing of Big Data. Spark is designed to use Hadoop MapReduce with some modifications that enable it to perform more efficiently. Apache Spark has its own streaming API and independent processes for continuous micro-batch processing across intervals with varying, but short time duration. Spark runs up to 100 times faster than Hadoop in certain circumstances. Spark has some features for real-time analytics and is supportive of applications such as machine learning, stream processing, and graph computation [Zaharia et~al(2012)Zaharia, Chowdhury, Das, and Dave]. MLlib is Spark's machine learning library, focusing on learning algorithms and utilities, including classification, regression, clustering, collaborative filtering, dimensionality reduction, as well as underlying optimization primitives. MLlib is built on Apache Spark, which is a fast and general engine for large scale processing that is up to 100x faster than Hadoop MapReduce, or 10x faster compared to disk. It supports Java, Scala, and Python.

4 Evaluation

4.1 Experimental Condition

An experiment was setup to investigate the performance of the machine learning algorithms with 128 different configurations, number of servers 3 through 10, and number of virtual cores 1 through 16 with data chunk size of 64 megabytes. The minimum number of servers needed to perform machine learning algorithms was selected to conform with the replication factor of 3 that refers to the storing of data on different machines.

4.2 Results

In the process of training the classification models we observed that the split rate of selected data for training data set does not effect the training time of the machine learning algorithms. This means that the only parameters effecting the training time of classification models for particular dataset and infrastructure are software parameters and the resources that are being used. We have discovered that the analysis won't complete if we don't provide enough RAM for the execution, and on the other hand adding excessive RAM will not increase the performance.

In this experiment we trained the logistic regression model with two LBFGS and SGD optimizers, with over 100 different configurations. The average training time of SGD was 207 seconds and average time of LBFGS was 106 seconds, as shown in Figure **1**, so we can conclude that logistic regression model can be trained 49 percent faster using LBFGS optimizer compared to SGD while being trained with similar cluster configurations.

As expected, it was observed increase in the performance of machine learning algorithms as the number of servers increased. It is noteworthy to state, however, that adding additional servers will increase the performance, but decaying performance with higher number of servers and adding these additional servers may outweigh the performance benefit. The results of this experiment is presented at Figure **2**.

We observed that having more than one virtual core makes significant difference in the training time and having 2 through 8 virtual cores performs equally well. Furthermore, increasing number of virtual cores used on each server to more than 8 degrades the performance of machine learning algorithm. We conclude optimum number of virtual cores is between 2 and 8, independent selected algorithm, next we compared training time based on number of servers.

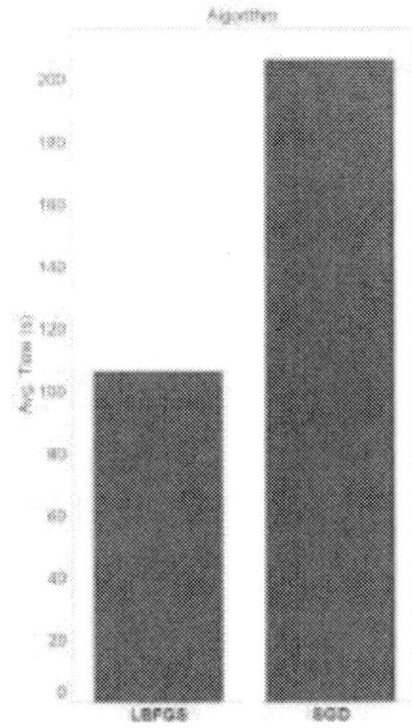

Figure 1. Comparison of average training time for logistic regression using SGD and LBFGS.

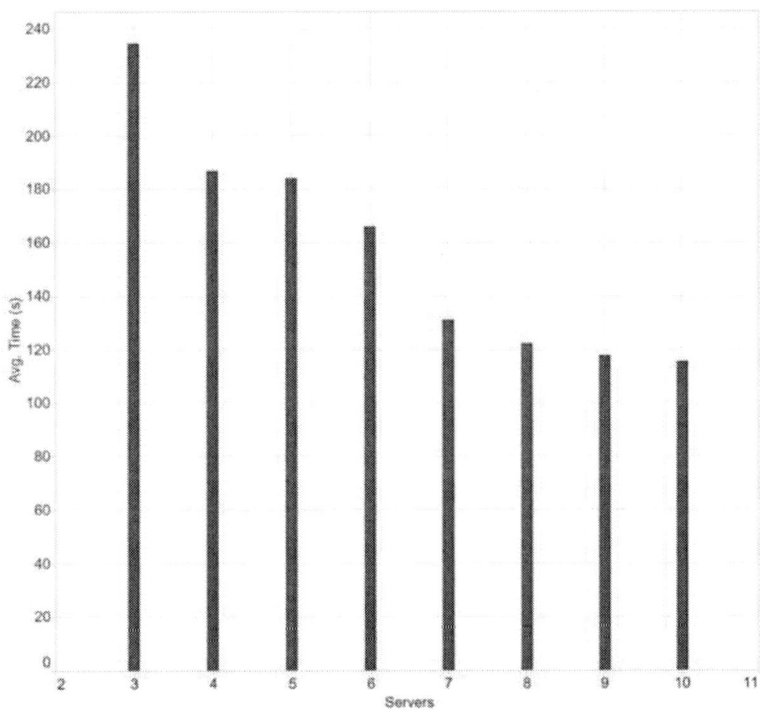

Figure 2. Time comparison of classification algorithms on different number of servers.

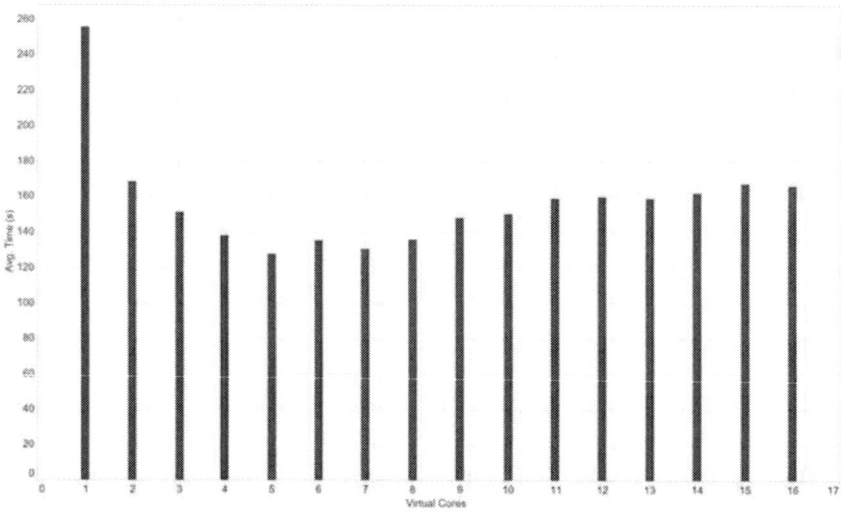

Figure 3. Comparison of average training time of classification algorithms per number of virtual cores on each server.

Interestingly, as shown in Figure **3**, the relationship between the number of cores and the performance of the machine learning algorithms did not follow a similar pattern to that of number of machines and performance. This issue raises concerns regarding Spark and YARNs ability to manage resources in training of machine learning algorithms.

We further analyzed results using tree ensembles and as was expected random forests capability to adapt with parallel processing; will allow training higher number of sub trees for training predictor model. Figure **4** shows the average training time for this algorithm using 5, 25 and 50 sub trees.

We Tested Gradient boosted trees with different number of iterations and as expected increasing number of iterations significantly increased its training time. Because of the iterative nature of this algorithm, parallelism and cluster computing only marginally helps with its boosting. As you can see in Figure **5** the training time of gradient boosted tree with even few iterations increases rapidly.

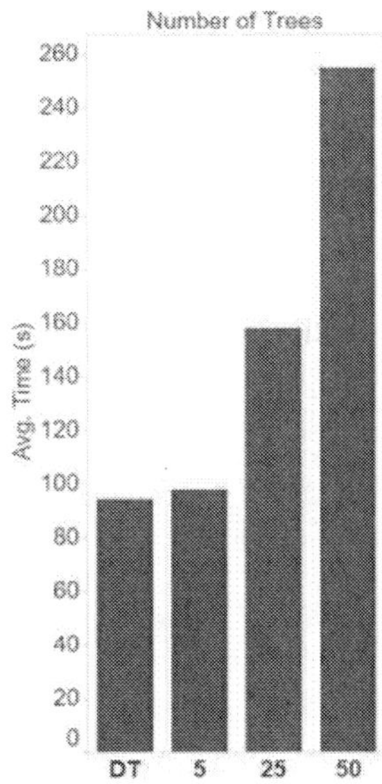

Figure 4. Training time Comparison of decision tree and random forests with 5, 25, 50 sub trees.

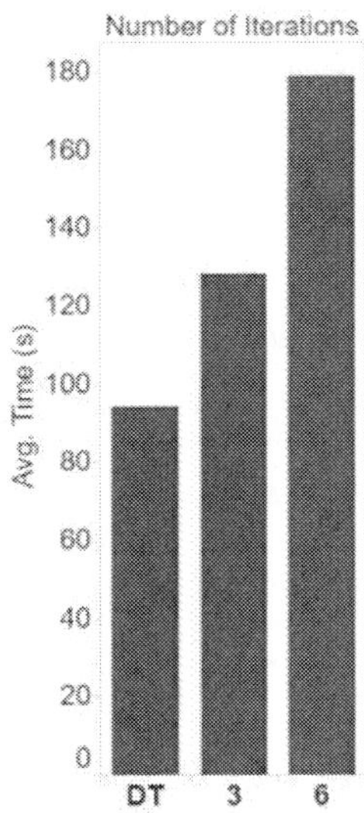

Figure 5. Training time Comparison of decision tree and gradient boosted trees with 3 and 6 iterations.

5 Conclusion

We have presented the optimal server and core configurations needed to best perform machine learning models using Apache Spark on a specific dataset. These optimal configurations will not only save time, but will also reduce cost of infrastructure. The performance of these machine learning algorithms were analyzed in regards to time in seconds. Factors such as number of cores, number of machines, and number of partitions were taken into consideration when analyzing the performance of the machine learning algorithms. It was discovered that as the number of servers increased, the performance increased as well, but performance however decreased, as the number of cores increased. These results infer that more servers and fewer cores are needed for optimal performance of machine learning algorithms. From a business perspective, it is best to use the number of machines that makes a significant impact on performance rather than a meager impact as means to save money. This justifies why we chose a number of servers that was less than the maximum amount of machines that were available. We wanted to maximize benefits and resources while minimizing expenditures.

Acknowledgements

This research was supported in part by Grant #1262933 and #1560037 from the National Science Foundation.

References

1. Acker O, Gröne F, Blockus A, Bange C (2011) In-memory analytics â€“ strategies for real-time CRM. Journal of Database Marketing & Customer Strategy Management 18(2):129–136, DOI 10.1057/dbm.2011.11
2. Ahn J, Yoo S, Mutlu O, Choi K (2015) PIM-enabled instructions. In: Proceedings of the 42nd Annual International Symposium on Computer Architecture - ISCA '15, ACM Press, New York, New York, USA, pp 336–348, DOI 10.1145/2749469.2750385
3. Apache Software Foundation (2015) Apache Spark - Lightning-fast cluster computing. URL http://spark.apache.org/
4. Baldi P, Sadowski P, Whiteson D (2014) Searching for exotic particles in high-energy physics with deep learning. Nature communications 5:4308, DOI 10.1038/ncomms5308 ,
5. Bärenfänger *et al*(2014)Bärenfänger, Otto, and Österle]Barenfanger2014 Bärenfänger R, Otto B, Österle H (2014) Business value of in-memory technology-Multiple-case study insights. Industrial Management and Data Systems 114(9):1396–1414, DOI 10.1108/IMDS-07-2014-0212
6. Cutler DR, Edwards TC, Beard KH, Cutler A, Hess KT, Gibson J, Lawler JJ (2007) Random forests for classification in ecology. Ecology 88(11):2783–2792, DOI 10.1890/07-0539.1

7. De'ath G (2007) Boosted trees for ecological modeling and prediction. Ecology 88(1):243–251, DOI 10.1890/0012-9658(2007)88[243:BTFEMA]2.0.CO;2
8. Deo RC (2015) Machine learning in medicine. Circulation 132(20):1920–1930, DOI 10.1161/CIRCULATIONAHA.115.001593 ,
9. Frenkiel2014 Eric Frenkiel (2014) Want to Rise Up in Your Organization? Real-Time Big Data Analytics Is the Wave to Catch - Database Trends and Applications. Database Trends and Applications 28(4):27
10. Garber L (2012) Using in-memory analytics to quickly crunch big data. Computer 45(10):16–18, DOI 10.1109/MC.2012.358
11. Garcia-Molina H, Salem K (1992) Main Memory Database Systems: An Overview. IEEE Transactions on Knowledge and Data Engineering 4(6):509–516, DOI 10.1109/69.180602
12. IBM (2017) What is In-memory computing. URL https://www.ibm.com/analytics/us/en/technology/data-warehousing/
13. Jin C, Kong Y, Kang Q, Qian W, Zhou A (2016) Benchmarking in-memory database. Frontiers of Computer Science 10(6):1067–1081, DOI 10.1007/s11704-016-5366-0
14. Kestelyn J (2013) Putting Spark to Use: Fast In-Memory Computing for Your Big Data Applications | Cloudera Developer Blog. URL http://blog.cloudera.com/blog/2013/11/putting-spark-to-use-fast-in-memory-computing-for-your-big-data-applications/
15. Khandani AE, Kim AJ, Lo AW (2010) Consumer credit-risk models *via* machine-learning algorithms. Journal of Banking and Finance 34(11):2767–2787, DOI 10.1016/j.jbankfin.2010.06.001
16. Kingsford C, Salzberg SL (2008) What are decision trees? Nature biotechnology 26(9):1011–3, DOI 10.1038/nbt0908-1011
17. Kumar S, Pandey MK, Nath A, Subbiah K (2016) Performance Analysis of Ensemble Supervised Machine Learning Algorithms for Missing Value Imputation. In: 2016 2nd International Conference on Computational Intelligence and Networks (CINE), IEEE, pp 160–165, DOI 10.1109/CINE.2016.35
18. Lee T, Lee KB, Kim CO (2016) Performance of Machine Learning Algorithms for Class-Imbalanced Process Fault Detection Problems. IEEE Transactions on Semiconductor Manufacturing 29(4):436–445, DOI 10.1109/TSM.2016.2602226
19. Sainani K (2006) Logistic Regression. PM&R 6(12):1–28, DOI 10.1001/jama. 2016.7653 ,
20. Samui2011 Samui P, Sitharam TG (2011) Machine learning modelling for predicting soil liquefaction susceptibility. Natural Hazards and Earth System Science 11(1):1–9, DOI 10.5194/nhess-11-1-2011
21. Siegal D, Guo J, Agrawal G (2016) Smart-MLlib: A High-Performance Machine-Learning Library. In: 2016 IEEE International Conference on Cluster Computing (CLUSTER), IEEE, pp 336–345, DOI 10.1109/CLUSTER.2016.49
22. Sopyła K, Drozda P (2015) Stochastic gradient descent with Barzilai-Borwein update step for SVM. Information Sciences 316(C):218–233, DOI 10.1016/j.ins.2015.03.073
23. Tan KL, Cai Q, Ooi BC, Wong WF, Yao C, Zhang H (2015) In-memory Databases. ACM SIGMOD Record 44(2):35–40, DOI 10.1145/2814710.2814717
24. Trajano AFR, Fernandez MP (2015) Two-phase load balancing of In-Memory Key-Value Storages through NFV and SDN. In: 2015 IEEE Symposium on Computers and Communication (ISCC), IEEE, pp 409–414, DOI 10.1109/ISCC.2015.7405549

25. Wang S, Summers RM (2012) Machine learning and radiology. Medical Image Analysis 16(5):933–951, DOI 10.1016/j.media.2012.02.005

26. Zaharia M, Chowdhury M, Das T, Dave A (2012) Resilient distributed datasets: A fault-tolerant abstraction for in-memory cluster computing. DOI 10.1111/j.1095-8649.2005.00662.x ,

27. Zheng2012 Zheng W, Bo P, Liu Y, Wang W (2012) Fast B-spline curve fitting by L-BFGS. Computer Aided Geometric Design 29(7):448–462, DOI 10.1016/j.cagd. 2012.03.004 ,

28. Zhou2017 Zhou L, Pan S, Wang J, Vasilakos AV (2017) Machine Learning on Big Data: Opportunities and Challenges, DOI 10.1016/j.neucom.2017.01.026

Using Classification Algorithms for Telemonitoring Parkinson's Disease Severity

Francisco Díaz-Pérez[1], Alfonsa García-López[1], Manuel Rubio-Sánchez[2], and Agustín Álvarez-Marquina[1]

[1] Universidad Politécnica de Madrid, Spain
[2] Universidad Rey Juan Carlos, Madrid, Spain

Abstract. There has been much recent research into the connection between Parkinson's disease (PD) and speech impairment. The findings prove the suitability of monitoring voice features, for tracking PD severity. *The Patient Voice Analysis Project* (https://www.synapse.org) is a public on line platform in which PD patients provide voice recordings and information about their symptoms. This platform has great potential to obtain large databases that, in addition to facilitate patient monitoring, help in PD research. The PVA data set consists of 779 remote, non-invasive, self administrated speech tests, with sustained vowel phonation, and self reported outcomes of Parkinson's Disease Rating Scale questionnaire. With this data set, we have used machine supervised learning classification algorithms for modeling PD severity (five classes) from voice recordings of patients. The best results for the multiclass classification problem have been obtained with a KNN algorithm and features selection. Results show how public telemonitoring platforms could facilitate large-scale clinical trials into novel PD treatments.

1 Introduction

Parkinson's Disease (PD), described in 1817 as "shaking palsy" by Doctor James Parkinson, is a neurodegenerative disorder of central nervous system that affects the control mechanism of the human body [6]. Given that age is an important risk factor for PD and the fact that the population is growing older, the prevalence of PD could rise bigger in the near future. At present there is no cure for PD, although medication may alleviate some of symptoms and improve quality of live for the patient. Early diagnosis and frequent tracking are important. Traditional methods, with clinical assessment, for monitoring Parkinson progression are expensive. Furthermore for PD patients physical visits to the clinic are very difficult. There is a need for inexpensive and objective clinical tool to track PD symptom progression. The development in information technology and telecommunication would offer a good opportunity for telemonitoring. In recent years the number of computer-based systems to provide diagnostic and monitoring support to clinicians has increased considerably.

People with Parkinson (PWP) suffer tremors, slowness of movement, rigidity and postural instability. But the early PD symptoms include disorders in the patient's voice. Research surveys conducted by the Parkinson's Disease Foundation state that more than 90% of PWP changes in their speech [10]. Furthermore there is empirical evidence for speech degradation as the disease progresses. Thus, analysis of vocal disorders can be an important medical procedure in diagnosing and monitoring PD.

Voice disorders can be measured by acoustic tools and there is a great deal of research for automatic the evaluation of pathological voice patterns [13, 17] and the analysis of their relation with PD [2, 4, 12, 18].

The following features of speech signals (dysphonia measures) have been measured in order to determine their influence on PD: Fundamental Frequency or Pitch, Shimmer, Jitter, HNR [4, 8, 11, 18]; Mel Frequency Cepstral Coefficientes (MFCC) [2, 20] and non linear dysphonia measures such as: Pitch Period Entropy (PPE), Detrended Fluctuation Analysis (DFA), Recurrence Period Density Entropy (RPDE) [7, 8, 18].

Some dysphonia measures are highly correlated with each other, which suggested the use of features selection methods [7, 8, 14, 19].

Sustained vowels have been found to carry more PD-discriminative information than the isolated word and short sentences do [11, 18].

Teixeira [16] proved that, in recorded sustained vowels, jitter parameters registered statistically significant differences between male and female voices. Furthermore Tsanas et al. [19] proved that there are substantially different PD effects in the voices of male an female.

Some previous studies used speech signals aiming to separate PWP from healthy controls [3, 4, 7, 20] or for discriminating PD of other neurological diseases [2]. Tsanas, Little et al. [19] used speech signal to determine PD severity and replicate a clinician's scale assessment. But this studio is limited by the number of patients (just 42).

There is various scales for monitoring PD progression. The Hoehn & Yahr Staging (H&Y) [5] is a severity index, which defines five broad categories of motor function in PD. The Unified Parkinson's Disease Rating Scale (UPDRS) is the most widely used for quantifying motor and non-motor symptoms severity [9]. The Parkinson's Disease Rating Scale (PDRS) is an abbreviated version of the UPDRS, that omits the clinical observation and measures the impact of PD in the day-to-day life of PWP. The PDRS questionnaire includes 17 questions, about memory problems, hallucinations/visions, mood, motivation, speech, excessive saliva, swallowing, handwriting, cutting food, dressing, hygiene, turning in bed, falling, freezing, walking, tremors and numbness. It can be self-administered and completed easily and quickly. Each question is rated on a (0-4) scale with 0 representing no disability and 4 worst disability. The PDRS score is the floor of the average score of the 17 items rescaled to [0-100].

In order to try to assess the PD severity of people from by their voice, well known statistical machine-learning algorithms can been used. Dysphonia measures are proposed as features (input variables) and the scores for a clinician's scale as output target variable. There are two main types of predictive modeling task: Classification, which usually is used for discrete target variables, and regression, which is used for continuous target variables.

Getting and processing voice recordings of PWP with research purposes is often an expensive process. Then public domain databases, accessible via the Internet, are very interesting, because they allow sharing data to different researchers. For instance, the UCI machine learning repository (http://archive.ics.uci.edu /ml/datasets/Parkinsons), with data of voice measurements of 31 people has been used in [3, 7] and [8]. Synapse (https://www.synapse.org/) is an open platform that data scientists can use to carry out, track, and communicate their research in real time. Synapse allows sharing scientific content (data, code, results). The Synapse project Patient Voice Analysis (PVA Challenge), is an effort to assess the severity and fluctuations in Parkinson's disease symptoms from voice recordings. In Synapse platform the patients themselves, through telephone calls, provide their voice recordings, give their demographic data and respond to the questions of the PDRS questionnaire. This project have great potential to obtain large databases that, in addition to facilitate patient monitoring, help in PD research. Currently the data set of PVA Challenge consist of remote no-invasive self-administrated test including: speech test with sustained voice phonations (3-30 seconds long), self-reported outcomes of PDRS questionnaire and a limited set of covariates with demographic information from 620 PWP. Elias Chaibud Neto and the PVA Challenge Dry Run Team have studied multiple predictive regression methods for the PDRS score with this data set. But only 2 of the top 10 ranking models used voice features. The best model is a randon forest, only employing the covariates data. The years since first symptom covariate has the strongest contribution to PDRS prediction. The little success of the regression models for predicting PDRS from voice features suggests try a classification models approach.

In this paper we present a study realized, with PVA data set and machine learning classification algorithms, which aim is to contribute to PVA project by analyzing the relationships between voice features and PD severity.

2 The Dataset

The PVA data files contain restricted data. Data access is governed by a set of procedures and principles designed to meet legal, ethical and regulatory standards for the sharing of coded human data.

The data set consists of 779 samples from 620 PWP (with some repeat calls) including:

- brief voice recordings of sustained vowel phonations (3-30 seconds),
- 38 features extracted from the voice recordings (see Table 1),
- self-reported symptom assessment (PDRS questionnaire as well as H&Y score),
- a set of covariates: age, sex, years since first symptom and on treatment indicator.

Table 1. Disphonia measures grouped into families of features

Label	Group	Features
$f_1 \dots f_5$	Pitch measures	F0 and its derivative, RMS power
$f_6 \dots f_{19}$	MFCC	Median cepstral coefficients 0-12
$f_{20} \dots f_{32}$	MCC derivatives	Time derivatives of MCC 0-12
$f_{33} \dots f_{35}$	Non linear measures	RPDE, DFA, PPE
$f_{36} \dots f_{38}$	Relative spectral power	0-500Hz, 500Hz-1kHz, 1-2kHz

2.1 Dataset Preprocessing

Before working on the data set, invalid and confusing data are removed. We have used a table with 739 records from 620 PWP (see Table 2).

Table 2. Covariates Overview

PWP	620
Age	Mean= 63.06, Median= 64, Minimum= 32, Maximum= 92
Gender	Male= 301, Female= 319
Years since first symptoms	Mean= 7.63, Median= 6, Minimum= 0, Maximum= 49
On medication	85%

As response variable we have discarded Hoehn & Yahr Staging, because is a severity index based purely on motor aspects and no motor symptoms are more relevant for PD clinical stage [1].

The PDRS questionnaire includes motor and non-motor symstoms. The distribution of the PDRS scores is fairly Gaussian, with $mean = 20.7997$ and $std = 11.0546$), (it pass the Kolmogorof-Smirnov test, at the 5% significance level).

To make a pure classification problem, each record has been targeted in a specific class according the PDRS score. Tsanas et al. [19] used classification algorithms to replicate UPDRS score, using a class for each UPDRS value. But we have categorized the values for PDRS just on five classes, because in this project the PDRS questionnaire has been self-reported, then the scores may not be accurate as they have not been tested by a clinician. Therefore, we have defined the target variable (PDRS-Classes) for the supervised learning classification process with the following values:

- Class 0: Completely independent, $PDRS \leq 11$ (179 records).

- Class 1: Difficulty for some works, $13 \leq PDRS \leq 17$ (144 records).
- Class 2: Slowly and difficulty, $19 \leq PDRS \leq 23$ (151 records).
- Class 3: Some dependence, $25 \leq PDRS \leq 30$ (132 records).
- Class 4: Disability, $PDRS \geq 32$ (133 records).

The histograms of PDRS variable and PDRS-Classes are shown in Figure 1.

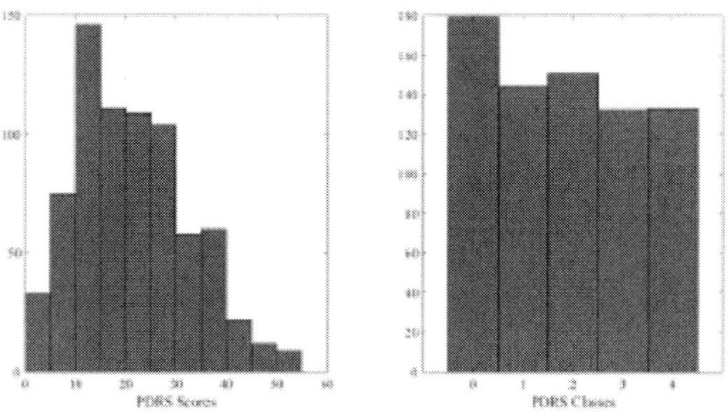

Fig. 1. PDRS variable distribution

3 Methodology

The methodology used in this study includes:

1. To analyze the data set and define the train matrix.
2. To explore correlation coefficients for doing a feature selection.
3. To use classification methods in a standard supervised learning setup.

As criteria for features selection we used correlation coefficients. For each group of features (see Table 1) first we choose the most relevant one to PDRS and after we compute correlation coefficients between different features to assess the extent to which they contain overlapping information. With the elimination of irrelevant and redundant features the aim is to improve the accuracy of the classification algorithms.

As classification algorithms (see [15] for details) we have used:

1. Decision tree (DT), with Gini index and different depths, MaxNumSplits= 30 or 40.
2. Support Vector Machines (SVM), with different kernels (Gaussian, lineal and cubic).

3. K-nearest neighbor (KNN), with different distances and different numbers of neighbors: 3, 5, 10.

All the classifiers have been experimented both, with features selection and without features selection.

Normalization has been employed to avoid features values in greater numerical ranges dominating those is smaller numerical ranges. For KNN algorithms the data are scaled to the interval $[0, 1]$, and for SVM algorithms the variables have been normalized to $mean = 0$ and $std = 1$.

Our approach assumes that the data set is a good representation of the overall data. Therefore, as validation procedure we use $resubstitution(p, q)$, where p and q are scalars between 0 and 1. The case $q = 1-p$ corresponds to holding out, while $p = q = 1$ corresponds to full resubstitution. After testing some possibilities we have chosen $p = 0.5$, $q = 0.9$. Then, for each proof a random selection of records is made for train (90%) and test (50%). Sets are selected in order to minimize the number of observations that are used in both sets.

All algorithms were implemented in MATLAB2016b©. We have made 200 runs on each model first with all the instances together and then with male and female instances separately.

We compared model performance on the basis of mean absolute error

$$MAE = \frac{1}{N}\sum_{i\in Q}|\widehat{y_i} - y_i|, \tag{1}$$

where $\widehat{y_i}$ is the predicted class, y_i the actual class, N the number of phonations in the test subset and Q contains the indices of that set.

For each model experimented, the MAE over the 200 realizations has been averaged and we have chosen the best classifier as the one with the highest rate of correctly classified instances (CCT).

4 Results

The train matrix has 739 rows (samples) the 38 features as predictors and the the categorized variable PDRS-Classes as response. After correlation coefficients analysis, the following 15 features are selected (see Table 1):

$f_1, f_4, f_7, f_{10}, f_{12}, f_{15}, f_{18}, f_{21}, f_{27}, f_{32}, f_{33}, f_{34}, f_{35}, f_{38}$.

Although in the voice features, significant differences have been identified for male and female, when an ANOVA test is applied, none of the models experimented have shown much better results when separately classifying sets of male and female.

Table 3 sumarizes the most significative results about performance of the classifiers, including the averaged MAE for each model and the highest rate of correctly classified test.

The presence of redundant attributes does not adversely affect the accuracy of decision trees. But DT algorithms have offered poor results with our database.

Table 3. Performance of classification models

Model	*MAE*	*CCT* (%)
DT, with 38 features and MaxNumSplits=40	1.047	51.49
DT, with 38 features and MaxNumSplits=30	1.115	46.88
DT, with 15 features and MaxNumSplits=40	1.086	48.24
DT, with 15 features and MaxNumSplits=30	1.161	44.44
KNN, with 38 features and 10 neighbors	1.293	41.91
KNN, with 38 features and 5 neighbors	1.149	48.53
KNN, with 38 features and 3 neighbors	1.031	55.83
KNN, with 15 features and 10 neighbors	0.309	87.50
KNN, with 15 features and 5 neighbors	**0.290**	**88.89**
KNN, with 15 features and 3 neighbors	0.287	88.08
SVM, with linear kernel and 38 features	1.292	40.38
SVM, with cubic kernel and 38 features	0.299	87.54
SVM, with Gaussian kernel and 38 features	0.343	87.80
SVM, with linear kernel and 15 features	1.383	34.96
SVM, with cubic kernel and 15 features	0.362	85.91
SVM, with Gaussian kernel and 15 features	0.629	75.88

Results of KNN algorithms clearly improved with feature selection, but not the same for SVM models.

The best performing for SVM algorithms has been achieved with cubic kernel without features selection. The best KNN classifier uses 15 features, Euclidean distance and 5 neighbors, the confusion matrix for this classifier is shown in Table 4.

Table 4. The confusion matrix for the best classifier

	Predicted 0	Predicted 1	Predicted 2	Predicted 3	Predicted 4
Actual 0	73	2	0	2	4
Actual 1	7	65	1	1	2
Actual 2	1	5	67	5	0
Actual 3	4	2	1	64	0
Actual 4	0	2	0	2	59

5 Conclusions

The speech sound samples of PD patients can be used as an input to a telemonitoring support system. This innovative approach facilitates remote tracking of disease progression, minimizing the need of regular visits to the clinic. Synapse project facilitates non-invasive remote tracking of disease progression and contributes to research by generating accessible data. As far we know, PVA data file consists of the public data set with the biggest number of patients. Despite possible lack of precision, due to the fact the test have been self-administered without medical check, the results prove that it is possible to estimate the severity of PD from the analysis of the vocal features collected on line. However, working with PVA data set we observed that the quality of the data itself limited the potential accuracy of the methods. For future work we propose to include quality control strategies in data acquisition. Improving the quality of voice recordings and PDRS questionnaire answers could bring better results in the performance of the classification models. In the other hand, undoubtedly the increase of the database would facilitate large-scale clinical trials in PD treatments.

Acknowledgments

This work has been partially supported by Spanish Ministry of Economy and Competitiveness (MINECO) Projet TEC2016-77791-C4-4-R. The authors would like to thank Ignacio Fernández Ocaña for his assistance in paper translation. We are pleased if this work could contribute the PVA project.

References

[1] Armañanzas, R., Bielza, C., Chaudhuri, K., Martinez-Martin, P., Larrañaga, P.: Unvealing relevant non-motor Parkinson's disease severity symtoms using a machine learning approach. Artificial Intelligence in Medicine 58, 195–202 (2013)

[2] Benba, A., Jilbab, A., Hammouch, A.: Discriminating between patients with Parkinson and neurological diseases using cepstral analysis. IEEE Transactions on Neural Systems and Rehabilitation Engineering 24(10), 1100–1108 (2016)

[3] Chen, H.L., Huang, C.C., Yu, X.G., Xu, X., Sun, X., Wang, G., Wang, S.J.: An efficient diagnosis system for detection of Parkinson's disease using fuzzy k-nearest neighbor approach. Expert Syst. Appl. 40(1), 263–271 (Jan 2013)

[4] Dixit, Mittal, V., Sharma, Y.: Discrimination of People with Parkinson (PWP) disease on the basis of voice parameter analysis. International Journal of Computer Applications 94(13), 9–14 (2014)

[5] Hoehn, M., Yarhr, M.: Parkinsoninsm: onset, progression and mortlity. Neurology 17, 427–442 (1967)

[6] Langston, J.: Parkinson's disease: Current and future challenges. Neurotoxicology 23(4-5), 443–450 (2002)

[7] Little, M.A., McSharry, P.E., Hunter, E.J., Spielman, J., Ramig, L.O.: Suitability of dysphonia measurementes for telemonitoring of Parkinson's disease. IEEE Transactions of Biomedical Engineering 56(4), 1015–1022 (2009)

[8] Peker, M., Sen, B., Delen, D.: Computer-aided diagnosis of Parkinson's disease using complex-valued neural networks and mRMR feature selection algorithm. Journal of Healthcare Engineering 6(3), 281–302 (2015)

[9] Ramaker, C., Marinus, J., Stiggelbout, A.M., van Hilten, B.J.: Systematic evaluation of rating scales for impairment and disability in Parkinson's disease. Mov. Disord. 17, 867–876 (2002)

[10] Roberts-South, A.: Improving communication in parkinsons disease, http://www.pdf.org/winter_14_comunication

[11] Sakar, B.E., Isenkul, M.E., Sakar, C.O., Sertbas, A., Gurgen, F., Delil, S., Apaydin, H., Kursun, O.: Collection and analysis of a Parkinson speech dataset with multiple tipes of sound recordings. IEEE Journal of Biomedical and Health Informatics 17(4), 828–834 (2013)
[12] Shirvan, R.A., Tahami, E.: Voice analysis for detecting Parkinson's disease using genetic algorithm and KNN classification method. In: 18th Conference on Biomedical Engineering, Theran, IEEE. pp. 278–283 (2011)
[13] Silva, D.G., Oliveira, L.C., Andrea, M.: Jitter estimation algorithms for detection of patological voices. EURASIP Journal of Advances in Signal Processing pp. 1–9 (2009)
[14] Soliman, A.B., Fares, M., Elhefnawi, M.M., Al-Hefnawy, M.: Features selection for building an early diagnosis machine learning model for Parkinson's disease. In: International Conference on Artificial Intelligence and Pattern Recognition (AIPR) IEEE (2016)
[15] Tan, P., Steimbach, M., Kumar, V.: Introduction to Data Mining. Pearson International Edition, New York (2006)
[16] Teixeira, J.P., Fernandes, P.O.: Jitter, shimmer and HNR classification within geneder, tones and vowels in healty voices. Procedia Techonology 16, 1228–1237 (2014)
[17] Teixeira, J.P., Oliveira, C., Lopes, C.: Vocal acoustic analysis- Jitter, shimmer and HNR parameters. Procedia Techonology 9, 1112–1122 (2013)
[18] Tsanas, A., Little, M.A., McSharry, P.E., Ramig, L.O.: Accurate telemonitoring of Parkinson's disease progression by noninvasive speech test. IEEE Transactions of Biomedical Engineering 57(4), 884–893 (2010)
[19] Tsanas, A., Little, M.A., McSharry, P.E., Ramig, L.O.: Nonlinear speech analysis algorithms mapped to a standard metric achieve clinically useful quantification of average Parkinson disease symptom severity. J. Royal Society Interface 8(59), 842–855 (2010)
[20] Tsanas, A., Little, M.A., McSharry, P., Spielman, J., Ramig, L.O.: Novel speech signal processing algorithms for high accuracy classification of Parkinson's disease. IEEE Transactions of Biomedical Engineering 59(5), 1264–1271 (2011)

Development of a Text-Based Classifier to Identify Immunology-Related NIH Grants

Fenglou Mao, Susan F. Cooper, Dawei Lin

Division of Allergy, Immunology, and Transplantation (DAIT), National Institute of Allergy and Infectious Diseases (NIAID), National Institutes of Health, Bethesda, MD
fenglou.mao@nih.gov, dawei.lin@nih.gov, coopersu@niaid.nih.gov

Abstract: The abstracts of all NIH-funded grants are publicly available *via* the NIH RePORT Expenditures and Results Tool (RePORTER) website and are a valuable resource to study trends in immunology research. To identify immunology-related grants, we have developed a text-based classifier, which is capable of analyzing a large number of abstracts to provide an objective numeric measure of the relevancy of each grant to immunology research. We collected more than 1,100 funded grants that had been reviewed by the NIH Immunology (IMM) Integrated Review Group (IRG), this set of grants served as the true positive data set. More than 1,900 NIH grants, funded after review by IRGs whose research focus was not immunology related served as the true negative dataset. The classifier was developed on this training dataset by using a Bayesian algorithm. The classifier developed two metrics, Edge-Ratio (r) and Average LIKE-score (S), with high discriminative power based on LIKE-score, a similarity score between all collected grants using their "Research, Condition, and Disease Categorization (RCDC)" signatures. RCDC is a computerized reporting process used by NIH since 2008 to categorize research topics for congressionally-mandated report purposes. For a given grant, the Edge-Ratio is defined as the percentage of non-zero LIKE-scores between this grant and all grants in the positive dataset. The Average LIKE-score is defined as the average non-zero LIKE-score between this grant and all grants in the positive dataset. A Naïve-Bayesian classifier trained by these two features had an overall prediction accuracy of 92.3%. A test of IMM grants funded from 2014 to 2015, which were not in the training sets, yielded a value of 80.1% accuracy.

1 Introduction

The National Institutes of Health (NIH) is the primary agency of the United States government responsible for biomedical and health-related research. In FY 2016, to accomplish its mission, 81 percent of the NIH's $32.3 billion budget was awarded as grants or contracts to more than 3,000 universities, medical schools, and other research institutions. Before award, each incoming application underwent peer review to evaluate its scientific merit.

Grant applications are reviewed within the Center for Scientific Review (CSR), which is organized into 25 Integrated Review Groups (IRG), each focused on a scientific discipline. Each IRGs is composed of a cluster of Scientific Review Groups (SRG), also known as study sections, each with a more defined scientific emphasis. CSR officers assign incoming applications first to an IRG and then to an SRG.

The officers at the CSR manually assign tens of thousands of applications submitted to NIH to study sections each year. The process implicitly embeds their understanding of the scientific classifications into the assignments. We hypothesized that key features of application text corpuses can represent those expert classifications, although some assignments might be ambiguous due to changes of sciences and human biases. In this pilot project, we have extracted text features that are most representative and used them to develop an automated and robust computer classifier that electronically screens applications and can identify those that are appropriate for the Immunology (IMM) IRG. The classifier can be a generic tool to classify if text contents such as journal or conference publications are relevant to the science defined by IMM IRG or not.

2 Materials and Methods

2.1 Training Set

We constructed a true positive dataset of 1,130 NIH grants that CSR officers had assigned to the IMM IRG from 2008 to 2013. A negative dataset of 1,900 NIH grants was constructed based on their assignment to 8 other IRGs that were related to medical research but did not focus on immunology. A summary of these grants is listed in Table 1.

Table 1. Grants in the training sets

Fiscal Year	Number of IMM Grants	Number of Non-IMM Grants
2008	125	343
2009	164	332
2010	121	311
2011	115	264
2012	129	297
2013	476	353
Total	1130	1900

2.2. Features

To construct a classifier that can differentiate IMM from Non-IMM grants, we used the NIH Research, Condition, and Disease Categorization (RCDC) system—a computer-based process that sorts all NIH applications into categories by research area, disease, or condition. As part of this process, RCDC electronically scans the text of specific sections of each grant application, identifies specific terms from a comprehensive thesaurus, and counts how often these terms appear. This produces an application signature that places the application into one or more RCDC categories.

By using the RCDC signature (terms and their weights), the LIKE-score *(d)* of any two grants can be calculated by using the dot products of the RCDC signatures of the two grants. The formula is summarized as follows:

$$d = \sum_{i} W1(i)W2(i)f(i)/100 \quad (1)$$

where i is the index of the shared terms between the two NIH grants; $W1(i)$ and $W2(i)$ are the weights of the term i of the first grant and second grant, respectively; $f(i)$ is another weight factor, which is called "Inverse Frequency." This factor is updated weekly as more applications are submitted to NIH, but it changes very slowly because the pool of NIH grants is very large relative to the number of incoming applications. RCDC signatures can be obtained from the NIH Query, View, and Report database.

Once we determined the LIKE-score of any two grants, we constructed a network of a large number of grants and extracted two features, Edge-Ratio(r) and Average LIKE-score(S), to be used in the classifier.

Given a group of grants G (reference group) and another grant g, the average LIKE-score, S, between g and G is defined as follows:

$$S = \sum_{i=1}^{N} S(i)/N \quad (2)$$

where i is the index of non-zero LIKE-score between g and another grant $g(i)$ in G; $S(i)$ is the LIKE-score between g and $g(i)$; N is the number of non-zero LIKE-score between g and G; and S is the average of non-zero LIKE-score between g and grants in G.

The Link ratio, r, is defined as follows:

$$r = N/N_0 \quad (3)$$

where N is the number of non-zero LIKE-score between g and G and N_0 is the total number of grants in G.

Both S and r provide a similarity measurement between g and G. A higher S value indicates a high LIKE-score between g and other grants in G, and a higher r value means g is similar to more grants in G.

2.3 Naive Bayesian Classifier

The WEKA Data Mining Software (1, 2) was used to create the classifier. By using the 1,130 IMM grants as G, we calculated S and r for all grants in the training set (both 1,130 grants in the positive set and 1,900 grants in the negative set). We tested multiple algorithms and the performance was comparable (see Section 3.2). We decided to use the Naive Bayesian method because of its simplicity and robustness. The overall accuracy (recall) in the training set was 92.3%.

The performance details of the Naive Bayesian classifier are in Table 2.

Table 2. Naïve Bayesian classifier performance

Class	TP Rate	FP Rate	Preci-sion	Re-call	F-Measu-re	MCC	ROC Area	PRC Area
IMM	0.867	0.043	0.923	0.867	0.894	0.835	0.973	0.950
Non-IMM	0.957	0.133	0.924	0.957	0.940	0.835	0.973	0.985
Weighted Avg.	0.923	0.099	0.923	0.923	0.923	0.835	0.973	0.972

3 Results and Discussion

3.1 Features Extraction and Comparison

In addition to the two features S and r, we also tested several other features to determine their ability to differentiate IMM grants from all grants in the training set. These features include the LIKE-score by itself, the total number of edges between g and G, and the LIKE-score sum of edges between g and G. The average LIKE-score and link ratio remained the best indicators of differentiation.

We also studied the effect on S and r when we changed the reference group G. The different G groups were as follows:

1. *G1:* All grants in the training set. S and r of this group can be treated as the background.
2. *G2:* All 1,130 grants from the IMM IRG . S and r of this group can be used as the similarity to IMM grants.
3. *G3_1; G3_2……G3_8:* The 8 negative subgroups from each of the 8 IRGs, the union of these groups forms the negative dataset *G3*.
4. *G2_1; G2_2; … , G2_12.* The 12 SRGs from within the IMM IRG

After comparing S and r under the different G scenarios, we reached the following conclusions:

1. *The S* and r values of the IMM grants and *G2* (IMM group) are significantly higher than the values between IMM grants and *G1* (the background). This confirms that IMM grants form a similar group, and the grants within this group are similar to each other.
2. *The S* and r values between IMM grants and *G2* is significantly higher than the values between IMM grants and *G3* (the negative set). This means S and r have the discriminative power to train a valid predictive tool.
3. S and r between *G3_1* grants and *G3_1* is significantly higher than values between *G3_1* grants and *G3_2* grants. This happens among other *G3* subgroups. This indicates these two features can also be used on other IRGs instead of just IMM.
4. S and r between *G2_1* grants and *G2_1* is similar with values between *G2_1* and *G2_2*, which means it is hard to use these two features to construct a predictive model to classify IMM subgroups (SRGs).

3.2 Comparison of Various Classifiers

After using multiple scenarios to study *S* and *r* values, we were confident that we had identified highly discriminative features for a classifier. We then used them to test various models of classifiers.

As the primary purpose of this study was to identify IMM grants from all NIH applications, we used *G2* as the positive set and *G3* as the negative set, and calculated *S* and *r* values for each grant in the training set by using *G2* as the reference group.

We list the accuracy (recall) rate of 8 different models in Table 3. The results show that the overall accuracy rate for the IMM group (positive set) is approximately between 82% and 89%; the overall accuracy rate for the Non_IMM group (negative set) is approximately between 92% and 95%; and the weighted accuracy rate is very close: approximately between 90% and 92%. This indicates that once features are selected, the machine learning methods do not differ significantly in their performance. In this study, we selected the Naive Bayesian method due to its simplicity and robustness, which allows the results to be more easily understood.

3.3 Test on Data by Fiscal Years

To test the performance of the Naive Bayesian classifier in a real-world situation, we conducted a study by using previous year's data as the training set and subsequent year's data as the testing data. Table 4 shows a summary of the results. For example, in 2008 there were a total of 468 grants in the training sets: 125 grants from the IMM IRG and 343 grants from other IRGs. We used these data to train a classifier, and obtained an accuracy (recall) rate of 80.8%, 94.2% and 90.6% for the positive, negative and whole sets, respectively; and then we used this classifier to predict the data from 2009 to 2013, in which there were 1,005 grants from the IMM IRG and 1,557 grants from the other IRGs. The prediction accuracy (recall) was 78.3%, 95.9% and 89.0% for IMM, Non_IMM and all grants, respectively.

Table 3. The performance of multiple classifiers

Classifier Name	IMM TP Rate	Non_IMM TP Rate	Weighted TP Rate
Naïve Bayesian	86.7%	95.7%	92.3%
SVM	82.6%	93.6%	89.5%
Multilayer Perceptron	89.4%	94.1%	92.3%
RBFNetwork	88.4%	94.9%	92.5%
BayesNet	88.7%	93.3%	91.6%
DecisionTable	88.1%	94.7%	92.2%
RandomForest	86.5%	92.2%	90.1%
Bagging	88.9%	93.6%	91.9%

The analysis shows that the accuracy of the model trained from FY 2008 only is lowest in both training and testing, which may be explained by having the lowest number of samples in the training set. For all other models, the accuracy is similar.

We can draw three conclusions from this analysis:

1. The model accuracy increases as the number of grants in the training set increases, but it becomes negligible when the sample number is big enough. In this study, this equates to between 500 and 1000 samples.
2. The model is robust because the blind testing shows a comparable accuracy with the training. Although the accuracy of the testing is slightly lower than the training, this is common in most data mining studies since the training set was used to develop the algorithm. An accuracy of 84% to 86% in training is considered similar to an accuracy 80% to 85% in real-world prediction.
3. The IMM grants remained quite stable from FY 2008 to 2013 since the model trained from previous years' data performed similarly for the following years data.

3.3 Robustness Test

To further test the robustness of the model, we conducted another study. We randomly picked *n* grants in the training set, and constructed the model, and calculated the accuracy. We repeated this process 100 times and calculated the average accuracy and standard de*via*tion of the accuracy. *n* was iterated from 10 to 3030 with an increment of 10. Figure **1** shows the changing of accuracy (for the positive set) and standard de*via*tion of this accuracy. As the number of samples (*n*) increased, the accuracy decreased and then became stable at about 86%. This pattern indicates that the model overfits the data when the number of samples is low; however, once n reached 200, the average accuracy reached the converged value. The standard de*via*tion converged much slower. 500 samples are needed to obtain 1% standard de*via*tion, and it continues decreasing while more samples added. Currently, we have 3,030 samples in the training set, and according to the robustness analysis, we can conclude that the model trained from this training set reaches 0.1% accuracy fluctuation.

Table 4. Testing by Fiscal Years (FY)

Trai-ning Set FY	IMM In Trai-ning Set	Non_IMM In Training Set	Accuracy In Trai-ning Set	Test Set FY	IMM In Test Set	Non_IMM In Test Set	Accuracy In Test Set
2008	125	343	80.8%,94.2%, 90.6%	2009-2013	1005	1557	78.3%,95.9%,89.0%
2008-2009	289	675	84.1%,94.1%,91.2%	2010-2013	841	1225	83.1%,96.5%,91.0%
2008-2010	410	986	85.1%,95.4%,92.4%	2011-2013	720	914	83.3%,96.3%,90.6%
2008-2011	525	1250	86.3%,95.9%,93.1%	2012-2013	605	650	85.5%,95.8%,90.8%
2008-2012	654	1547	86.5%,95.9%,93.1%	2013	476	353	82.6%,96.9%,88.7%
2008-2013	1130	1900	86.7%,95.7%,92.3%	2014-2015	166	3611	80.1%,93.4%,92.8%

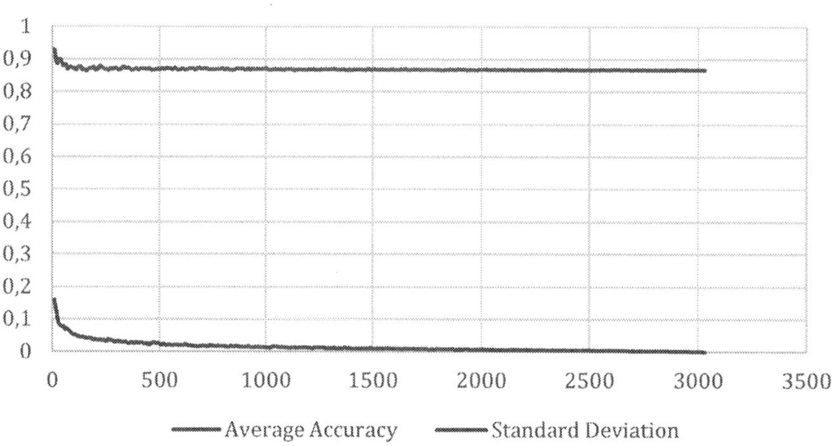

Figure. 1. Bayesian Classifier Robustness Analysis.

3.4 RCDC Terms Coverage

Because our method uses RCDC LIKE-scores between NIH awards, we also wanted to know more about the RCDC terms within the subset of the IMM awards. We had 1,130 samples in the positive set, which included 6,600 unique RCDC terms. These had different weights and were found with high frequency in many awards. We used formulas (4) and (5) below to calculate the RCDC terms ratio, *r(t)* :

$$n(t) = \sum_i W(i,t)f(t) \tag{4}$$

$$r(t) = \frac{n(t)}{\sum_t n(t)} \tag{5}$$

where *t* is the index for *t*th RCDC term; *i* is the index for the *i*th award in the positive set; *W(i,t)* is the weight of the *t*th RCDC term in the *i*th award; *f(t)* is the "Inverse Frequency" of the *t*th RCDC term, which is a constant for each RCDC term; *n(t)* is the contribution of *t*th RCDC term among all awards in the positive set; and the RCDC term ratio *r(t)* is the normalized value of *n(t)* among the positive set.

We randomly picked a subset of these 1,130 samples, generated the RCDC terms of this subset, and then summed their RCDC term ratio *r(t)*. Figure **2** shows the trend as the sample size is increased. When the sample size is 170, the sum of the weighted RCDC term ratio reached 85%; it reached 95% when the sample size was 500.

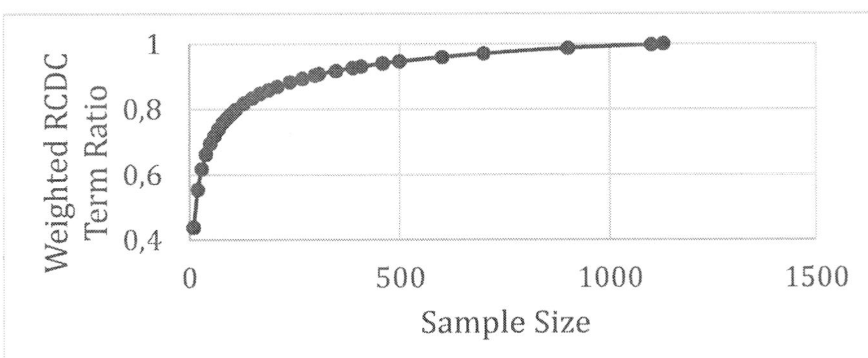

Figure 2. RCDC terms coverage vs. sample size.

3.5 Subject Matter Expert IRG Reassignment Test

Officers at the Center for Scientific Review (CSR) assign submitted applications to an IRG based on their judgment as to the best scientific fit. A Principal Investigator (PI) has the right to request their application be assigned to a specific IRG. Occasionally, an application might cover a topic(s) that could place it in more than one IRG. All these variables make the IRG assignment challenging and inexact. Consequently, our training data set may not be 100% accurate.

However, one advantage of our method is that it does not require the training data to be 100% accurate since the two features (*S* and *r*) are determined from a large number of grants; therefore, the classifier can tolerate some error in the sample data. To further test the effectiveness of this model, we manually picked 289 grants (we specifically introduced bias by selecting more grants predicted wrong by the model) and asked two NIAID subject matter experts (SME) to manually review the abstract of all grants. The SMEs classified each grant as an immunology grant or not. Table 5 shows a summary of the results.

Table 5. IRG Re-assignment Test

CSR IRG Assignment	Total	Predicted IRG by the classifier	Predicted Number	SME IRG Reassignment	Strongly Agree	Weakly Agree	Hard To Decide	Total	Ratio
IMM	158	IMM	70	IMM	56	0	0	56	80%
				Non_IMM	11	3	0	14	20%
		Non_IMM	88	IMM	47	8	1	56	64%
				Non_IMM	30	1	1	32	36%
Non_IMM	131	IMM	79	IMM	23	1	2	26	33%
				Non_IMM	44	7	2	53	67%
		Non_IMM	52	IMM	0	0	0	0	0%
				Non_IMM	52	0	0	52	100%

In the category of CSR-assigned IMM grants, the SME reassignment to the IMM IRG agreed with our classifier assignment 80% of the time. The SME reassignment had a 36% agreement with our predictions for a grant to be a Non_IMM grant, which indicates our model can identify about one third incorrectly assigned IMM grants based on expert opinion. Another observation was that if a CSR IMM grant is predicted as a Non_IMM grant, the SME had a greater uncertainty at the reassignment: in a total number of 56 grants assigned to IMM, 9 of them were "weakly agree" or "hard to decide." In the category of CSR assigned Non_IMM grants, if our model predicted them as IMM grants, the expert assignment was 33% in agreement and demonstrated that our model can re-capture about one third of the IMM grants that were incorrectly assigned to other IRGs by CSR. We noticed that that the uncertainty was increased if the model prediction and the expert assignment disagreed with each other. If the model predicted a CSR assigned Non_IMM grant as Non_IMM, the expert assignment agreed 100% with the prediction. This suggests that if both CSR and the model agree that a grant should be Non_IMM, there is no need for human curation.

3.6 IRG Prediction for R01 Applications to 10 NIH Institutes (IC)

We applied the classifier to R01 applications that were submitted to 10 NIH Institutes (ICs) during FY 2014. We selected these 10 ICs because they received a large number of applications, many of which were immunology related, e.g., NIAMS. As anticipated, the classifier predicted that NIAID had the highest percentage of incoming applications for the IMM IRG (see Figure **6**). NIAID was followed by the much smaller NIAMS that supports research into several immunologic diseases such as arthritis, psoriasis, and atopic dermatitis. NCI, NIDDK and NHLBI were next at about nine percent each. These ICs support immunological research, for example immunotherapy to treat various kinds of cancer and the study of autoimmune diseases such as diabetes. The remaining five ICs received negligible IMM-like applications due to the focus of their research portfolio not being strongly linked to immunology or immunology-related areas. The predicted percentages of each IC's IMM-directed applications seems to be intuitively consistent with their research priorities.

The actual CSR assignment of applications to IMM from NCI, NIDDK and NHLBI is around 1 to 2 percent (not shown), which is much lower than our classifier predicts ~9 percent. This is consistent with our finding in 3.6 above, in which our Subject Matter Expert IRG showed that approximately one third of the IMM grants predicted by our tool were assigned to a non_IMM by CSR.

Table 6. IMM/Non_IMM prediction on 10 NIH Institute/Center(IC) applications in 2014

IC Name	Number of R01 applications	Predicted as IMM	Predicted as Non_IMM
NIAID	2261	835 (36.9%)	1426 (63.1%)
NIAMS	730	91 (12.5%)	639 (87.5%)
NCI	3514	326 (9.3%)	3188 (90.7%)
NHLBI	2579	238 (9.2%)	2341 (90.8%)
NIDDK	1800	164 (9.1%)	1636 (90.9%)
NIA	940	47 (5.0%)	893 (95.0%)
NINDS	1976	93 (4.7%)	1883 (95.3%)
NEI	969	41 (4.2%)	928 (95.8%)
NICHD	995	25 (2.5%)	970 (97.5%)
NIMH	1504	22 (1.5%)	1482.(5%)

3.7 Prediction of IMM Grants in Other IRGs

We also ran the prediction program on grants to other non-IMM IRGs from 2008 to 2014. Table 7 shows the number and percentage of IMM and Non_IMM grants identified by the classifier.

Table 7. Prediction of IMM/Non_IMM for all type 1 R01 in 2008-2014

IRG	Predicted_As_IMM	Predicted_As_Non_IMM	Percentage
IMM	676	179	79.06%
OTC	151	1071	12.36%
IDM	142	782	15.37%
AARR	142	787	15.29%
CVRS	115	980	10.50%
DKUS	97	592	14.08%
CB	87	1033	7.77%
MOSS	84	829	9.20%
BDCN	83	1273	6.12%
VH	66	662	9.07%
OBT	51	985	4.92%
BST	47	740	5.97%
EMNR	47	823	5.40%
SBIB	41	974	4.04%
MDCN	33	1063	3.01%
BCMB	28	949	2.87%
GGG	25	924	2.63%
PSE	25	1098	2.23%
IFCN	20	945	2.07%
BBBP	8	788	1.01%
RPHB	8	851	0.93%
HDM	8	908	0.87%
ETTN	6	203	2.87%
IMST	4	88	4.35%

The analysis shows that IMM IRG has the highest number of predicted IMM grants (676), and it also has the highest percentage (79.6%) of predicted IMM grants. Both results are as expected and confirm that the method of the classifier met our initial goal.

The 5 IRG (OTC, IDM, AARR, CVRS and DKUS) below the IMM IRG had between 151-97 predicted IMM grants (15.37%-10.5%.) These values can be rationalized based on the scientific scope of these IRGs. (For example, the Oncology 2 - Translational Clinical IRG (OTC) considers "applications involving translational and clinical investigations that encompass cancer prevention, diagnosis and treatment". Some of these cancer studies are immunology related.)

However, the remaining IRGs all contained some predicted IMM grants, ranging from 1% to 9%. This might indicate that there are a number of IMM grants that are misplaced and merit further assessment.

4 Conclausion

In this study, we constructed a Naive Bayesian model to identify basic immunology grants from all NIH grant applications. Two RCDC-LIKE score derived features were designed to train the model. Both features are network based and we verified the robustness of the model in multiple tests.

In the testing by fiscal years, the model performed well when we used previous years' grants as a training set and the following years' grants as a test set. This indicates that basic immunology topics did not change much, or only very slowly, over the last few years.

When we applied the model to applications from other NIH ICs the results highlighted a potential issue of IMM grants not being directed to the IMM IRG.

We leveraged the 1,130 IMM grants in the training set to predict future NIH grants as IMM or Non_IMM. The 1,130 grants provided a signature able to identify future NIH grants or even other medical research text as immunology related.

Acknowledgements

This study is supported by NIAID/DAIT. We want to acknowledge Gabriel Rosenfeld and Quan Chen for their helpful discussion. We also want to thank Thomas Esch, Lara Miller, Wolfgang Leitner, Travis Hauguel and Charles Hackett who manually reviewed the grants.

References

1 Eibe Frank, Mark A. Hall, and Ian H. Witten (2016). The WEKA Workbench. Online Appendix for "Data Mining: Practical Machine Learning Tools and Techniques", Morgan Kaufmann, Fourth Edition, 2016.

2 Mark Hall, Eibe Frank, Geoffrey Holmes, Bernhard Pfahringer, Peter Reutemann, and Ian H. Witten (2009). The WEKA Data Mining Software: An Update. SIGKDD Explorations, Volume 11, Issue 1, June 2009, pages 10-18.

Industry 4.0: Mining Physical Defects in Production of Surface-Mount Devices

Farshid Tavakolizadeh[1], José Ángel Carvajal Soto[1], Dávid Gyulai[2] and Christian Beecks[1]

[1]Fraunhofer Institute for Applied Information Technology Schloss Birlinghoven, Sankt Augustin, Germany, farshid.tavakolizadeh@fit.fraunhofer.de, angel.carvajal@fit.fraunhofer.de, christian.beecks@fit.fraunhofer.de
[2]Institute for Computer Science and Control, MTA SZTAKI, Kende u. 13, Budapest, Hungary, david.gyulai@sztaki.mta.hu

Abstract: With the advent of Industry 4.0, production processes have been endowed with intelligent cyber-physical systems generating massive amounts of streaming sensor data. Internet of Things technologies have enabled capturing, managing, and processing production data at a large scale in order to utilize this data as an asset for the optimization of production processes. In this work, we focus on the automatic detection of physical defects in the production of surface-mount devices. We show how to build a classification model based on random forests that efficiently detects defect products with a high degree of precision. In fact, the results of our preliminary experimental analysis indicate that our approach is able to correctly determine defects in a simulated production environment of surface-mount devices with a MCC score of 0.96. We investigate the feasibility of utilizing this approach in realistic settings. We believe that our approach will help to advance the production of surface-mount devices.

Keywords: Industry 4.0, surface-mount technology, data mining, classification.

1 Introduction

A *surface-mount device* is an electronic device with components mounted on the surface of printed circuit boards (PCBs). The method for production of surface-mount devices is called the *surface-mount technology (SMT)*. This method consists of three steps: solder pasting, component pick and place, and solder reflow. SMT has enabled manufacturers to reduce the volume, weight, and cost of electronic devices.

The increasing demand in surface-mount devices has resulted in considerable advancement in SMT production systems [1, 2]. Yet, the generation of defects remains inevitable due to a number of factors such as machinery failure, bad parts, and imperfect production process. Common physical defects are missing solder paste and solder bridge in the solder printing step; missing and falsely oriented parts during pick and place phase; and faulty solder joints and component shift in the solder reflow step [1]. Occurrence of defects increases costs and deteriorates the SMT manufactu ring process [3].

Defect detection of surface-mount devices is mostly attributed to physical properties. These properties can be inspected with a combination of vision-based and data mining methods. In this work, we present the SMT process through a realistic simulation. Considering the real-time constraints and unlikelihood of defects, we evaluate the effectiveness of random forests in mining defects. Furthermore, we study the feasibility of utilizing the algorithm in a closed production feedback loop to save manufacturing costs.

This paper is structured as follows. Section 2 outlines related work. Section 3 details the utilized production environment. We propose our classification approach in Section 4. The results of the performance analysis are given in Section 5 before the paper is concluded with an outlook on future work in Section 6.

2 Related Work

Several works focus on detecting surface-mount defects during and after the production. Kim *et al.* [4] present a system that extracts solder joints from images and trains neural networks classifying defects with 98% accuracy. Ko *et al.* [5] propose a X-ray system using linear vector quantization and multi-layer perceptions to detect defective *ball grid array* solder joints. Acciani *et al.* [1] extract regions of interests from images of surface-mount boards and use similar algorithms to detect solder joint defects with an accuracy of 98.8%. Tsai and Yang [6] present an eigen-based similarity measure for finding deviations from a reference image to detect flaws in PCBs and components placement. Hui and Pang [2] propose a method to detect solder paste defects by 3D reconstruction of solder profiles, geometric segmentation, and classification with full accuracy. In another work, authors present DMAIC [3] to improve the solder pasting process and reduce defects by 44%.

Maier *et al.* [7] propose a general purpose system that uses probabilistic deterministic timed automata to learn the topology of production components and their behavior. Subsequently, it detects anomalies by comparing new entries with the learned models. Another work [8] presents a distance-based classification method for anomaly detection in real-time after an offline training phase.

Previous works present systems suitable for detection of different kinds of defects on surface-mount devices. While [1, 2, 4, 5, 6, 8] show outstanding results, none offer a methodology that adapts to changes in product specifications. These systems typically rely on a training set acquired at an offline phase and assume that the training set applies to all new products. In addition, [1, 4, 5, 6] solely consider images taken from products and do not take into account data collected by other means (e.g. non-visual sensor measurements). On the other hand, [7] learns adaptively from production data and performs accurate defect detection. However, because the approach only models process information, it is unlikely that it will be successful in SMT classification. In production of surface-mount devices, most defects occur due to deviations in physical properties of devices [1, 2, 4, 5, 6]. In this paper, we focus on physical properties of surface-mount devices and present elements of an adaptive classification system.

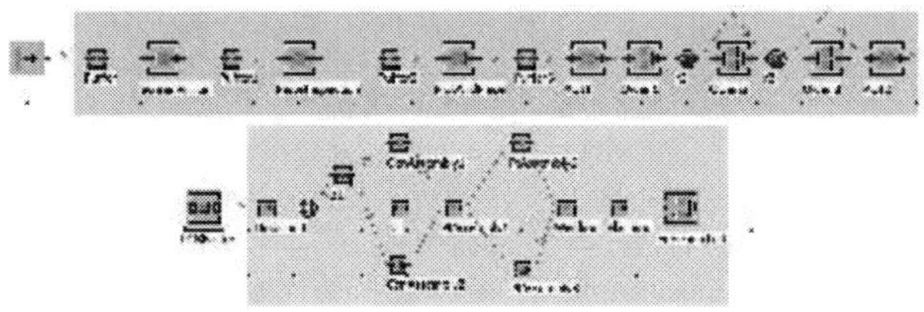

Figure 1. Layout of the SMT (top) and Non-SMT (bottom) assembly lines.

3 SMT Production Environment

We created an environment using Siemens Tecnomatix Plant Simulation [9] that mimics the material flow and production processes performed in an actual SMT production line. The use of simulation enables us to understand the SMT process control without accessing and interfering with a running factory.

The environment consists of two assembly lines interconnected *via* an in-process buffer. The first line is fully automated, responsible for all steps of the SMT method. The second line performs operations related to assembly of machanical components (e.g. springs, screws, and connectors) and functional inspections. In this line, several stations are operated by humans and parallelized for an optimized throughput. Figure **1** shows the layout of both assembly lines. On the first line, production items are transported from one station to the other using a belt conveyor system, whereas they are conveyed manually in the second line. Furthermore, a buffering mechanism is in place between several stations to compensate for variations of the time needed for different operations. Table **1** describes the stations.

Table 1. Description and total measurements produced by each of the stations.

Station	Description	M.
ScreenPrinter	Pastes solder on designated areas of the PCB using a stencil	2
PasteInspection	Optically checks if solder correctly covers the solder pads	12
PickAndPlace	Picks components and places them on specific positions	4
AOI	Automated optical inspection: checks position of components	12
Oven	Reflows the solder paste so that components mount to the PCB	1
Housing	Placement of the surface-mount device in a plastic housing	1
ConAssembly	Mounting Non-SMT connectors on the PCB and/or housing	2
PtAssembly	Assembly of other components (e.g. springs, auxiliary modules)	2
Welding	Closing the lid of the housing with high-frequency welding	1
Flashing	Flashing firmware on the Chip(s)	0
FunctionTest	Performing final quality inspections on products	1

The environment manufactures six types of surface-mount devices $P_1, \dots, P_6$ with similar product layouts. In this way, each product P_i is mapped to a mathematical feature vector $x_i \in \mathbb{R}^{53}$ as follows:

$$P_i \rightarrow x_i = (d_1, \dots, d_{42}, \tau_1, \dots, \tau_7, t_1, \dots, t_3, \nu) \in \mathbb{R}^{53} \quad (1)$$

Each feature vector x_i comprises four types of measurements that are recorded for each product: the spatial coordinates of the solder joints and the surface-mount components $\{d_j\}_{j=1}^{42}$, the torques applied for tightening screws $\{\tau_j\}_{j=1}^{7}$, the temperatures in reflow ovens $\{t_j\}_{j=1}^{3}$, and the welding frequency for mounting the housing components ν. Moreover, each product is given a label, based on the functional test performed at the end of the production. On average, 5% of products fail the functional test.

4 Random Forests Classifier

Random forests [10] is an ensemble learning method that works by constructing multiple decision trees during the training and taking an aggregation of their outputs for each classification task. The use of multiple decision trees makes random forests less prone to overfitting and more robust on imbalanced datasets.

We simulated the production of 30768 products of type P_1 and utilized [11] to aggregate sensor measurements during the production. For each generated product, we extracted a feature vector $x \in \mathbb{R}^{53}$ with a label and stored them together in a database. We performed simple dimensionality reduction to map identical measurements from parallel production station into one feature. This enabled us to make the dimension of feature vectors uniform regardless of the production process. All other numeric measurements were used directly as features, in total resulting in feature vector $x' \in \mathbb{R}^{51}$.

We tried various parametrization of the algorithm to find the optimal configurations for high accuracy and short training time. The result was an ensemble with 100 trees and max depth of 90 for each tree. In addition, as in [10] we set the maximum number of features used for training of each tree to $log_2 M + 1$ where M is the dimension of x'. Other parameters such as minimum number of samples required to split an internal node and a leaf node were set to 2 and 1 respectively per [12]'s recommendation. During the training we allow the growth of a tree until all its nodes reach an impurity of below 10^{-7} or the tree exceeds the max depth threshold.

To evaluate the effectiveness of the ensemble with the suggested settings, we trained a model with 90% of the dataset selected at random. The model was trained in 26 seconds and achieved a Matthews correlation coefficient (MCC) score of 0.96 on the remaining 10% of the data. We chose MCC for evaluating the performance because it considers the weight of classes and also reflects true/false positives and negatives. In a class-wise comparison, the classifier detects 94% of defects and wrongly classifies non-defects at a rate of 3×10^{-4}.

5 Experiments

We showed that a random forests model trained with a large dataset can accurately classify most defects. However, in realistic settings, it is not always feasible to manufacture that number of products in a reasonable amount of time. In another experiment, we continuously re-train the model over a growing dataset; see Figure **2**. The MCC score is close to 0.9 when trained with about 5000 vectors and well above 0.9 after 8000 vectors. The fraction of falsely classified items (Hamming Loss) goes below 0.01 with more than 7500 vectors.

During the production, the items go through subsequent stations responsible for different tasks. A classification mechanism is practical only if it is able to detect a defect in a short time window after leaving a station and before it is placed on a track toward the next station. We closely monitored the production process and realized that this time window is at least 6.57 seconds. On average, the classification using the presented approach takes 110 milliseconds to complete (Powered by Intel W3565 @3.20GHz and 8GB of RAM). This leaves us with a remaining 6.46 seconds for transfer of data from and back to the production line.

The suggested classifier achieves an Accuracy (ACC) of 98.4% when trained with a balanced dataset of 2000 feature vectors. We balanced the data because ACC measure does not consider the weight of classes but it is required for comparison with the related work.

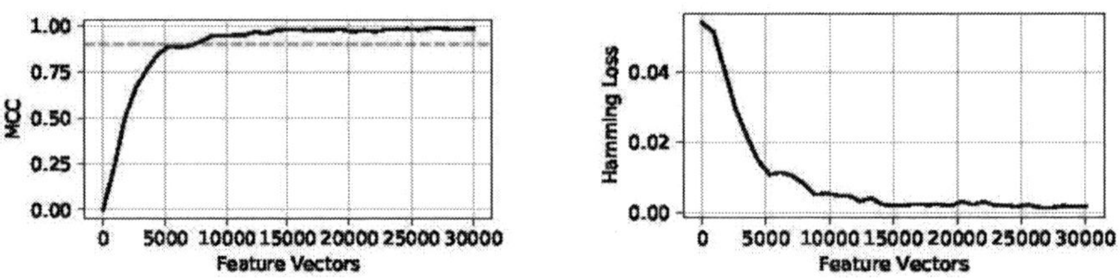

Figure 2. The performance of the classifier with respect to total feature vectors available during the training.

6 Conclusions and Future Work

In this work, we defined and presented a realistic production process. We simulated the process with state-of-the-art technologies, creating a data mining testbed. We showed that it is feasible to train accurate models in such an environment while fulfilling real-time constraints. Altogether, those parts constitute the building blocks for constructing and proving the feasibility of an adaptable stream mining framework applying state-of-the-art machine leaning techniques in real-time and online. To do so, the following future work is foreseen:

1. Integrating the classification system with the production environment using existing protocols and standards.
2. Collecting the data in an efficient and scalable manner.
3. Providing an adaptable framework that fits into Industry 4.0 needs.

4. Investigating the application of interactive machine learning techniques [13].
5. Offering a flexible, integrated, and manageable solution to data scientists allowing them to work in industrial settings effectively and realistically.
6. Evaluating the benefits of such systems from a manufacturing perspective.
7. Finally, validating the approach in real-world use cases.

Acknowledgements

This work is supported by the European Commission through the H2020 projects EXCELL and COMPOSITION under grant no. 691829 and 723145 respectively.

References

1. Acciani, G., Brunetti, G., Fornarelli, G.: Application of neural networks in optical inspection and classification of solder joints in surface mount technology. IEEE Trans. on Industrial Informatics. 2(3), 200–209 (2006)
2. Hui, T., Pang, G.: Solder paste inspection using region-based defect detection. The International J. of Advanced Manufacturing Technology. 42(7-8), 725–734 (2009)
3. Li, M., Al-Refaie, A., Yang, C.: DMAIC approach to improve the capability of SMT solder printing process. IEEE Trans. on Electronics Packaging Manufacturing. 31(2), 126–133, (2008)
4. Kim, T., Cho, T., Moon, Y., Park, S.: Visual inspection system for the classification of solder joints. J. Pattern Recognition. 32(4), 565–575 (1999)
5. Ko, K., Roh, Y., Cho, H., Kimn, H.: A neural network approach to the inspection of ball grid array solder joints on printed circuit boards. IJCNN. 5, 233–238 (2000)
6. Tsai, D., Yang, R.: An eigenvalue-based similarity measure and its application in defect detection. Image and Vision Computing. 23(12), 1094–1101 (2005)
7. Maier, A., Vodencarevic, A., Niggemann, O., Just, R., Jaeger, M.: Anomaly detection in production plants using timed automata. ICINCO. 363–369 (2011)
8. Toth, D., Aach, T.: Improved minimum distance classification with Gaussian outlier detection for industrial inspection. Image Analysis and Processing. 584–588 (2001)
9. Siemens PLM: Plant Simulation. https://www.plm.automation.siemens.com/en/about_us/index. shtml (Visited on 2016-12-10)
10. Breiman, L.: Random forests. J. Machine learning. 45(1), 5–32 (2001)
11. Soto, J.A.C., Jentsch, M., Preuveneers, D., Ilie-Zudor, E.: CEML: Mixing and moving complex event processing and machine learning to the edge of the network for IoT applications. IoT 2016. 103–110 (2016)
12. Louppe, G., Holt, B., Arnaud, J., Hedayati, H.: Random Forests. Scikit-learn: Machine learning in Python. http://scikit-learn.org/stable/modules/generated/sklearn.ensemble.RandomForest Classifier.html (Visited on 2017-03-15)
13. Saket, B., Kim, H., Brown, E. T., Endert, A.: Visualization by Demonstration: An Interaction Paradigm for Visual Data Exploration. IEEE Trans. on Visualization and Computer Graphics. 23(1), 331-340 (2017)